GHOSTS OF
ROSS COUNTY,
OHIO

GHOSTS OF ROSS COUNTY, OHIO

NEAL PARKS

HAUNTED
AMERICA

Published by Haunted America
A Division of The History Press
Charleston, SC
www.historypress.com

Copyright © 2024 by Neal Parks

All rights reserved

Cover images by Neal Parks.

First published 2024

Manufactured in the United States

ISBN 9781467155694

Library of Congress Control Number: 2024937573

CONTENTS

Contents

Acknowledgements

Where should I begin? To start off with, I am beyond grateful for the love, support and help from my brilliant and beautiful wife, Kristin; my talented and amazing son, Lucas; and my equally talented and hysterical daughter, Isabella. Thank you to my parents for years of support and encouragement; my mother-in-law for the early days of editing and her constructive criticism; and my family, friends, fans and followers for the years of your support and for always showing up at random book signings, conventions and festivals, no matter how far away they were. Your love for me and what I do has not gone unnoticed. Thanks to the Lord for the gift of art, literature and dogs. Thanks to my acquisitions editor, John Rodrigue of The History Press/Arcadia Publishing. Thanks to Wheatberry Books, Yolanda Harris, *The Morning Blitz* on 99.7FM and *Good Day Columbus* on ABC6. If anyone reading this feels overlooked or unappreciated, I am very sorry and I will do better next time.

The House in Brewer Heights

Chillicothe's history holds many myths, secrets and mysteries. The neighborhood of Brewer Heights on the west end of town is no exception. There are hundreds of homes occupied by just as many families within this neighborhood. According to many of the residents in this neighborhood, several of the homes have had strange and unusual happenings occur there. With so many of these houses built into the hillside, atop the rolling hills and a few among them at the base of the hill, I had to narrow this story down to only one house along this street. This specific house is said to have hosted the most paranormal occurrences, more than any other home in Brewer Heights. I will not be revealing the family's name or address in order to protect their privacy. One of the first encounters this family shared with me happened in 1998.

The Guest

Brooke was walking from the kitchen back to the living room. Footsteps could be heard following behind her. She stopped walking and slowly turned her head. She saw her boyfriend standing at the edge of the walkway from the kitchen.

"Terry? When did you come in? I didn't even know you were here." Terry stood there, silent and motionless. He grinned menacingly and started

The entry. *Neal Parks Photography*.

walking slowly toward her. Brooke was stunned as Terry went from a fully formed person to a black, smokey mass and then disappeared. She was jolted by the experience, shifting from being excited to see Terry to being enveloped by fear. Brooke wasted no time running through the hall back into the living room, where her family were sitting.

"Brooke? Are you okay, sweetie? Who were you talking to in there?" Brooke's mother, Marsha, said to her. She stood there in front of them, sweaty palms, racing heart and a lump in her throat.

"D-D-Did-did Terry come in here earlier or has he been here at all?" Brooke asked. Her parents sat there in silence just staring at her.

"Brooke, honey, Terry hasn't been here since he dropped you off from your classes this afternoon. Why do you ask?" The words escaped Brooke—

The overlook. *Neal Parks Photography*.

she couldn't produce a sound at first. She took a deep breath and loudly replied, "I saw him! He was just here, then he disappeared! He just vanished right in front of me!" Her back tightened and her legs stiffened. Her mother quickly stood up and walked toward Brooke. She embraced her with a hug and pulled away to lock eyes with her. She escorted Brooke into the foyer and quietly said to her, "Brooke! That wasn't Terry that you saw. Since we moved in here last year, I've seen things in this house too."

Brooke's head started to spin. She grabbed onto the buffet near where they were standing. "What? What have you seen?" Brooke asked.

"I've heard footsteps in the hallway, voices in the kitchen when I'm alone, shadows along the walls and a foggy-looking human form moving in and out of the guest room," she replied. After her mother shared her experiences with Brooke, a small statue that was sitting on the piano slid from one side of the top to the other and then fell to the floor as they were talking. Brooke grabbed her mother and held tightly to her.

"Does dad see it too?" she asked her mother.

"He says that there's nothing in this house other than us, but he finds that sort of thing ridiculous. Don't worry, sweetie. I have a feeling that whatever is happening here doesn't have any ill will towards us," Brooke's mother said lovingly.

The Dinner Party

A few days passed with no other strange occurrences, which was great for Brooke's nerves. Her father was out of town on a fishing trip with friends, and her mother was catching up with old friends late in the day. Brooke made it a point to spend as little time as possible at home alone. She intentionally stayed longer after her college classes and studied in the library—sometimes with friends, sometimes with her boyfriend. It was getting close to dinner, and she knew that her mother would be home soon; the chances of her being alone in the house would be slim. Brooke started to gather her books and notes, said her goodbyes to her study group and headed to the parking lot.

"What took you so long, Brooke?" Terry asked as she was heading to her car. He was leaning against his car in the best James Dean he could attempt. Brooke's eyes lit up when she saw him. She had been so busy with studying and talking to her friends that she hadn't taken the time to call or send him an email. They had plans for dinner with Brooke's mom at her house. She felt better knowing that there would be so many people at her house. She feared being alone there after her experience. Brooke and Terry hugged, and then she gave him a very long and heavy kiss.

"Wow. You are in a great mood. What did I do?" Terry asked. Brooke playfully smacked him in the arm and then leaned into him. They got in their vehicles and headed to her house for dinner. Upon entering her home, Brooke and Terry were met with the amazing aroma of pasta and freshly baked Texas toast. "Mom! We're finally here!" Brooke announced their arrival.

"Greetings kids! I'm in the kitchen!" her mother said.

"This all smells amazing as always, Mrs. Hall!" Terry said aloud. Brooke's mother turned to see Brooke and Terry standing in the kitchen with their eyes enlarged and mouths watering.

Greetings. *Neal Parks Photography*.

"Flattery will get you everywhere, Terry," Brooke's mother said jokingly.

"Oh my God, mom! That sounds so gross!" Brooke exclaimed. Her mom threw a kitchen towel at Brooke. "Swing and a miss, Mom! Work on that!" Brooke said. Terry laughed as he took Brooke's hand. He led her to the dining table and sat her down.

"Let me get your plate for you. You deserve it," he said to Brooke.

"Wow, Brooke baby. Your dad won't even do that for me anymore. I guess I'm old hat now," Brooke's mother said. Terry helped to set the table and pass out drinks. Brooke and her mother looked at each other and just smiled, knowing that the other was thinking about how kind and nice of a person Terry was and how beyond helpful he was every time he visited.

"Don't skimp on the pasta sauce, Terry!" Brooke said to him as he was getting her plate of Italian deliciousness together. She was waiting for her mother and Terry to take their seats. Something pulled her attention away from the moment. Brooke noticed a strange, smokey figure standing in the middle of the hallway leading to the bedrooms. She dropped her fork, which alerted her mother to what was transpiring. "Mom!" Brooke whispered raspily. "What is that?" she continued.

Her mother noticed almost immediately after Brooke dropped her fork. "Yes, honey. I see it." Terry turned to see what they were staring at. Floating in the middle of the hallway was something in human form, but it was a thick, dark mist.

"What? What is that? Brooke? What is that?" Terry said. He reached for her hand as she stood up to back away from the table.

Brooke's mother moved toward the apparition. "What are you? Who are you? Do you need our help?" she asked the entity. Brooke's eyes widened, and Terry grabbed her by the hand to steady her. He didn't know what to do or how to help. He was just as shocked and scared as Brooke.

As quickly as it appeared, it soon dematerialized. A few seconds after that, two upright vacuums and a canister vacuum rolled out into the middle of the hall from the front of the storage closet. This was followed by Brooke's bedroom door slamming shut on its own, and then Brooke's mother's door slammed shut. A few long seconds of deafening silence passed as they all stood in the kitchen just staring down the hall and then at one another.

"I can't be in this house right now, Mom! This is becoming too much!" Brooke said to her mother. Grabbing her books and some personal items, she went to walk out of the door and leave this haunted nightmare behind until she was stopped by Terry.

"Brooke! I don't know what this thing is, but you can't let it win. Your family owns this house and everything that comes with it! Stand your ground and don't let it run you out of here. I will stay here with all of you. You're not alone in this." She began to cry as she buried her head into his chest. He embraced her and held her tightly. Brooke's mother entered the room.

"That sounds like a novel idea, Terry. It's your choice and I thank you. I can prepare the guest room for you, or you can sleep on the couch." Marsha said to Terry.

He responded, "The couch would be ideal. I'm not interested in that guest room at this point in time."

Marsha laughed and playfully nudged Brooke. "Ha! Big brave man going to keep us safe from the ghost?" she said as she laughed. Terry hung his head as they all chuckled.

It Comes at Night

This was the first night in a while that Marsha was able to fall asleep right away. Her husband, however, never had a problem with sleeping. She would often stare daggers in his direction because of his ability to just drift away

Looming overhead. *Isabella Parks Photography*.

to dreamland. The temperature in the room changed suddenly. The subtle sound of a child giggling filled the air and woke Marsha. Her eyes opened, and she stared at the ceiling in frustration.

What is that? she thought to herself. Marsha turned to look at Robert, who of course was sleeping like the dead. The giggling sound started again. It sounded like a faint echo fading in and out of range. She sat up in bed suddenly and peered deeply into the darkness. Marsha was attempting to make sense of what she was hearing and allow her eyes to adjust.

"Hello?" she whispered aloud. It was still and silent. Marsha looked over at her husband as he continued to sleep through all of it. Her eyes were starting to adjust to her surroundings, which were shrouded in darkness. Marsha's stomach dropped when she noticed to the right of her bed, next to her closet, a partially solid and semitransparent form of a woman holding a very small boy.

The two of them were not a normal color. They looked like a sepia tone from an old image. Marsha gathered herself and said aloud, "May I help you?" She thought to herself, *"May I help you?" What was that, Marsha?* She continued to observe what was happening in front of her. The mystery woman was dressed in clothing from what appeared to be the 1930s. Her hair was half up and half down. Hairpins were tightly bunched together, with each strand pulled to their limit. The ghostly woman was holding the child close to her and smiling as she playfully lifted him higher then slowly lowered him as they laughed together.

Marsha was awestruck. She turned to look at her husband again, but he was still sleeping. As she looked back in the direction of where she saw the apparition, she was shocked to see that the woman was now looking directly at her. *Why is she looking at me?* Marsha said to herself. The ghostly woman was freely floating, her feet barely touching the floor as she hovered in front of Marsha.

"Who are you? What do you want?" she asked the phantom intruder. The woman didn't utter a word. She slowly turned her entire body with the small boy still in her arms. The hair stood up on the back of Marsha's neck. She said to the silent specter, "You are more than welcome to be here, too, just like us. Please, just let us rest."

"Ahhh! Who is that?" Marsha's husband shouted. The ghostly woman and child faded away like a mirage. Robert was more than awake at this point.

Marsha turned to him and said, "Oh would you calm down! It's just the other people who live here that I've told you about! Now do you believe me?"

Robert turned on the lamp next to him and sat all the way up in bed to look around the room. He was shaking and pale, and he grabbed Marsha's hand. "You weren't just imagining things or fooling around? What you've told me is real?" Robert asked Marsha. She started to smile and laugh a little at the image of the big man he's always carried himself as being. "I woke up because I thought you were talking in your sleep!" Robert exclaimed.

"Well, suffice it to say you've been formally introduced to our unseen housemates." Marsha replied. After that experience they shared together, Marsha and Robert slept for the remainder of the night in the family room with a few lights on.

The weeks turned into months and the months into years. The family continued to experience paranormal activity and have strange encounters. One day, after Brooke graduated from college and moved into her own place, Marsha decided to do her own research on the property where her home was built, as well as the history of the neighborhood before people moved in. She had heard stories from people in the area about how a lumber company set up campsites along the hillside and at the top of the hill for workers and their families while they worked to clear out the area around one hundred years ago. It's said there was an accident involving a horse-drawn wagon overloaded with lumber heading up the hill. The hitch snapped, and the wagon careened down the hillside and through the campsites. Dozens of women and children were killed or injured before the wagon stopped.

This was during a time in history when immigrants were doing the work and their families came with them to live, go to schools and set up their lives in the New World. If you died during this time, with no next of kin to claim your body and no money for a proper burial, you were normally buried where you died or in a mass grave. Upon learning this information, Marsha felt at peace, as she understood why these things were happening in her home and who these people were. She didn't feel alone in this. There were other homes in the neighborhood affected by paranormal activity, and Marsha had a better understanding of what might be causing it.

The Ghost of Lindy Sue

Y ou look beautiful tonight, Lindy Sue," Clem said as he nervously placed his hands in his coat pockets. Lindy Sue Buchanan was hailed as the most beautiful girl in the town of Knockemstiff. She was one of those girls the guys stood up for as she entered a room, the kind of girl other girls wanted to be like. Her father was a wealthy businessman, and her mother kept their house in order and would venture into town to make her presence known. They were a powerful family, well established not just in town but in the tri-county region.

"Thank you, Clem. You look very handsome," Lindy Sue replied. Clem Fiffe was a hard worker and a brilliant builder. He had been courting the young Lindy Sue for a while and already had the talk with her father—the important talk that so many men before him would have had with the fathers of their brides to be. "I'm surprised it's this warm in late September. It was a perfect day, and now it's a gorgeous night," Lindy Sue said to Clem. He extended his hand and helped her into the carriage.

Clem had plans set up around the area for their carriage ride. He was taking her to the lake for a ride in his rowboat and a small picnic. "Lindy, I'm going to take you on a small boat ride so we can watch the sun set." Upon hearing this, she was filled with giddy delight. The atmosphere around them was crisp with fresh autumn air. They had expected it to be chilly on this day, but to their surprise, the jackets that they brought were not needed. They approached the lake as Clem brought the horses to a steady stop so he could set up for their walk to the boat. Lindy Sue held Clem's arm as they started

The calling. *Kristin Parks Photography.*

on their short jaunt. Clem noticed an enormous footprint in the mud near the edge of the lake. "What is that?" he said as they stopped suddenly.

"That's the biggest footprint I've ever seen," Lindy Sue replied. The footprint appeared to be twice as long as the normal size of a man's print and a lot wider. They decided to just brush it off as nothing and just put it behind them. She was helped into the boat by Clem, and he started the push into the water.

"Oh my goodness, this water is cold!" he exclaimed.

Lindy Sue laughed and replied, "Hurry! Get into the boat!" As he started to row and the boat began to move, their eyes locked and Lindy Sue's smile spoke volumes. A light breeze cut through them as they enjoyed the scenery. It was eerily silent as Clem continued rowing.

"Do you feel like we are being watched?" Lindy Sue asked Clem. He felt the same way but was not willing to admit it. He wanted to put her mind at ease.

"Oh no. It's just all of the animals out here. They're everywhere." Clem said to her. He was hoping that would calm her nerves. As they approached the part of the lake where he planned for them to just sit and talk a little, he handed a fresh pear to Lindy Sue.

"You know I love pears, Clem. Thank you very much." She took the pear and held it with both hands. She looked up at him and said, "This view is so beautiful. I've been here many times before, but this time feels perfect." Clem was happy with her reaction and certain that she was able to relax.

The mood felt almost too perfect. Clem was preparing to move closer to Lindy Sue when their attention was suddenly pulled away from the moment and directed toward some movement coming from the nearby tree line. "Who is that?" Clem asked puzzlingly. They watched the stranger in the foliage crouch down and hide behind two trees.

"How tall is that man?" Lindy Sue said. She grabbed tightly to Clem's hand. He placed his arm around her in the hopes of comforting her. Whatever they saw slowly stepped to the right of the trees and crouched down behind some large bushes and a boulder. "Where did it go?" Lindy Sue asked. Clem noticed that after it lowered itself out of sight, you could still see the thing's head and part of its face. He wasn't sure if he should tell Lindy Sue or keep that information to himself.

Clem felt that it was time for them to take the boat back to the carriage. The two of them remained quiet as Clem rowed feverishly. He went from smiling at Lindy Sue to keeping an eye on the tree line. As they approached the carriage, the horses acted nervous. Something had obviously spooked them. Clem pulled the boat in, soaking his shoes and the legs of his trousers.

"Take my hand, Lindy. I think it's time to go now." Clem said to her as he pulled Lindy Sue out of the boat and quickly led her to the carriage.

"What did you see Clem? You're really scaring me!" Lindy Sue said to Clem, shaking nervously. Clem didn't respond at first. He grabbed the reins of the horses and snapped with authority.

"Yaw! Go!" Clem said to the horses in a commanding voice. He turned to look back at the tree line as they pulled away from the lake. Clem saw the thing that had been watching and following them earlier. It was gigantic in comparison to some of the shorter trees. "Lindy Sue! Stare straight ahead. Don't look behind us. Whatever you do, don't look back there!" Clem said to her as the thing behind them started to walk faster in their direction. Clem gave the reins another snap and called out to the horses to move faster. Lindy Sue didn't listen to Clem's request. She couldn't help herself, looking over her shoulder and seeing what was chasing them. It was taller than a bear and wider than a full-grown red oak tree.

"Oh my God! What is that?" Lindy Sue screamed aloud. Clem looked directly at her, out of ideas to keep her calm. The horse-drawn carriage had never moved so fast. The harder Clem pushed the horses, the closer the giant creature approached.

The bridge that sat over the creek was getting closer. Clem felt that once they reached the bridge, they would be safe. Lindy Sue started to cry and held tightly to Clem's arm. He turned to look back at the creature and noticed that it was gone. They finally reached the bridge, and Clem pulled back and stopped the carriage. The horses were breathing heavily as Clem grabbed his rifle from under the seat. He stood up and turned to face where he last saw the thing. He panned the area with his rifle positioned in his shaky hands.

"Clem. What was that thing?" Lindy Sue asked.

"I don't know. I've never seen anything like that," he replied. The atmosphere grew silent. A light breeze started to cool the air, followed by an ungodly odor. Lindy Sue started to gag from the horrible stench. She grabbed the reins and used them to pull herself up so she could get a better look at where the beast might be hiding.

Suddenly, the beast towered over them as it pulled itself up from the side of the bridge. Its fur was matted and stringy, its eyes were black as coal and the facial features were obscured by more fur. The creature blocked out what remained of the sunset. Clem lifted his rifle and fired a shot into the thing. The sound of the rifle startled the horses, and they jerked forward. Lindy Sue was holding on to the reins and lost her balance. She fell forward, causing the reins to wrap around her neck. The sudden movement led to Clem falling out of the carriage and onto the ground. As the carriage began careening away from the scene, the beast lunged at Clem and grabbed him by the neck and leg. Clem was still holding on to his rifle and placed the barrel into the neck of the beast. The gun went off and kicked against Clem's chest—the sounds of cracking bones echoed through the valley. Clem's screams were soon silenced by the beast as it knocked him off the bridge and bashed Clem's frail body into the creek below. Lindy Sue's body lay on the ground after she had fallen out of the carriage. Her life was tragically taken much too soon.

To this day, legend says that the spirit of Lindy Sue haunts the valley of Knockemstiff. Many people have reported seeing her ghost while walking the bridge or driving past the area. Several people have experienced car trouble as they drive over the bridge. Locals have talked about hearing screams in the area. Through the years, a few houses have been built near the bridge, and people have reported seeing a giant creature near the creek bed, by the pond and along the tree lines. Were these things and sightings all connected to the elusive creature that was following the two of them? Was her death an accident caused by this encounter? The fact behind this legend is that Lindy Sue was found dead, strangled, on the bridge over Paint Creek early one morning after she and her boyfriend, Clem, had taken their buggy through the area. Her death was tragic and left a hole in the heart of this valley. The horses were found days later, said to have died from fright, and the buggy was smashed. Clem was never seen again. No one knows what really happened, but like all ghost stories and legends, we are sometimes forced to draw our own conclusions.

CRYBABY TUNNEL

T he tunnel on Schrader Road, also known as Crybaby Tunnel, rests on the outskirts of Chillicothe, where East Main Street becomes Charleston Pike. According to legend, a distraught woman placed her infant on the railroad tracks and left it for dead. The baby was run over and killed by a train. Many people have said that if you drive through the tunnel at night with your lights off and windows down, you may hear the cries of the baby. One of the other versions of the story says that the mother and her newborn were walking on the tracks above the tunnel during a heavy storm when a train came barreling toward them. The mother was forced to toss her baby into the creek in an attempt to save its life; unfortunately, both the mother and the baby were killed.

Many people have reported that you can see the mother's ghost and hear the baby crying at night. The ghost of a woman who was murdered supposedly haunts the tunnel as well. Her body was discovered inside a waterbed mattress on the banks of Lick Run Creek at the north end of the tunnel. Many people have reported seeing her in the area. Cold spots, weird feelings and vehicle batteries dying have been reported in the tunnel, and several witnesses have reported seeing strange, glowing balls of light and shadows moving in the darkness.

It was a warm November when Mike and his friends decided to explore the tunnel on Schrader Road. "Do we really have to do this so late and in the dark?" Mike's girlfriend, Jill, asked. He chuckled lightly as he looked into the rearview mirror and at his friend Nick. The car full of friends coasted down the road in search of the legendary tunnel.

Crybaby Tunnel. *Don O'Brien*.

"Isn't this the tunnel where a woman placed her infant on the railroad tracks and left it for dead?" Nichole asked.

Jill chimed in and said, "That's not what I've heard. My dad told me that years ago the mother and her newborn were walking on the tracks above the tunnel during a heavy storm. The rain was coming down so hard that the mother didn't see or hear the train until it was too late. She had to toss her baby into the creek and try to save its life, but both of them were killed." The car grew silent after that story.

Nick spoke up, "Well, that's a wonderful story. Who's ready to see a ghost baby?" The group of friends started to laugh, which changed the somber mood after that brooding tale.

Nichole leaned into Nick and said, "How long do you think this will take?"

Nick locked eyes with her, conveying a look of disappointment. "I thought you would find this to be cool," he said to Nichole. She shrugged her shoulders and smiled begrudgingly as she reached for Nick's hand. Mike had to turn on his bright lights as the road got darker. The trees along the road created a canopy that blocked out the natural glow of the moon. The car full of friends continued on their journey to the enigmatic tunnel.

"How far is this place Mike?" Jill asked.

Nick chimed in, "I bet he's taking us out here to kill us!"

Nichole elbowed him, laughed and said, "Maybe you'll die slowly Nick." He gave Nichole a look and leaned into her to steal a kiss. She met him halfway and kissed him first. "Okay you two! I can see that in my rearview!" Mike said in an attempt to keep the car windows from fogging up.

Mike decided to share a story that Jill told him about the tunnel that she heard from a friend. "Her friend Kaycie went to the crybaby tunnel late one night. Her sister, Lacie, brought a couple of friends with them. Lacie's friend claimed to have seen a dark figure with red eyes. Kaycie said that her sister's friend said that the dark figure would move every time that she would blink her eyes. Kaycie said that she had seen a flash of light in the other tunnel, but her sister didn't see anything at all."

Jill laughed and said, "If you're going to tell my story, try not to leave other stuff out, dork! Kaycie also said that she saw a ghostly woman looking at them and pointing. They didn't know if it was some kind of warning. She wasn't smiling—she looked angry. They ran to the end of the tunnel and looked back, but she was gone."

Nick started to laugh and said, "Did you believe even a little bit of that?"

Jill looked at him with a scowl on her face and responded, "Don't shoot the messenger, jerk! I'm only sharing a story!"

As they turned a corner, the sign for Schrader Road shined brightly from the headlights of the car. They pulled up to the tunnel slowly and turned off the headlights. Mike rolled down his window and looked out over the creek near the tunnel. "So, did the baby die in the creek bed?" he asked.

Nichole gasped and said, "That's a bit morbid, Mike! Geez!" Jill turned around and looked at Nichole. They couldn't help but burst out in laughter. Along the walls of the tunnel, graffiti had been sprayed from top to bottom. Some of the names, words, phrases and messages appeared to have been there for the last one hundred years.

"This is like some kind of time capsule," Mike said. While making their rounds back and forth, Nick started knocking on the side of the tunnel. He was tapping and slapping along the wall.

"What are you doing Nick?" Jill asked.

"I've heard that there is a weird hollow area near the middle of the tunnel where an opening used to be, but they sealed it over." Nick replied.

"Who's 'they' Nick? That's a little vague," Nichole said. As Nick continued to knock again, he found a weird spot on the wall with the words "Boo" repeatedly spray-painted over it. There was a weird hollow sound coming from that spot. Although the rest of the tunnel was solid, this area was different.

"Hail Satin?" Mike said aloud as he was reading the graffiti.

"What did you say?" Nichole asked.

Mike laughed and said, "These jokers can't even spell Satan. They sprayed the word *satin* instead." The group laughed and started to look around for more misspellings and funny messages. The wind began to pick up and whipped through the tunnel. It started to feel very chilly, and a strange sound started to fill the air.

"I'm not joking right now guys! Does that sound like someone crying or moaning?" Nick asked the group. The group of friends remained still and silent as they listened to their surroundings. All of them heard it, except for Mike.

"Are you guys lying or making the noise yourself? I don't hear a thing!" Mike said angrily. They walked back and forth in the tunnel for a few minutes until they heard the noise again. This time, Mike heard it. "Is that an owl?" he asked.

The rest of the group looked at him. "An owl? Dude, really? An owl?" Nick replied. Jill and Nichole laughed and then walked together in the same direction toward the car. Mike was fumbling with his keys as the group was heading toward the car. It was locked but still running.

"I've heard that you're supposed to shut off your vehicle and put it in neutral, then it moves on its own like someone is pushing it." Nick said.

"Oh my God! Don't you dare!" Jill pleaded. Everyone took their seats and closed their doors. Mike made eye contact with Nick. With a smile on his face, Nick mouthed the words, "Do it!" Mike rolled down the windows, put the car in neutral and shut off the vehicle.

"Why are you turning off the vehicle?" Jill asked.

Nick laughed and responded, "The baby won't cry if the car's running."

Nichole smacked Nick's arm and said, "Oh my God! Shut up!"

Mike gripped the steering wheel tightly, took a deep breath and shouted, "I killed your baby!"

Jill jumped out of her seat, pushed Mike angrily and screamed, "Oh my God! What is wrong with you? Why would you say that?" She kept hitting and smacking his arm as he laughed hysterically.

"Okay. Okay. Okay! We'll go. We will go!" Mike said. He proceeded to start the vehicle, but it wouldn't turn over. *Click. Click. Click.*

"Stop fooling around Mike! Start the car!" Nichole screamed. Mike kept trying, but the car wouldn't start. Something smacked the outside of the car, near the back of the car. A sudden push was felt, and the car started to slowly roll on its own. The girls in the car became unhinged. They were screaming so much that their eyes filled with tears.

"Dude! Mike! Put the car in park; it's in neutral! It won't start in neutral! Put it in park!" Nick shouted after realizing that the car was not in the correct gear. Mike grabbed the gear shift, applied the brake pedal and pushed the shifter into park. He was finally able to start the vehicle, then he immediately shifted into drive and accelerated like a runaway train.

"You better get us home alive you jerk!" Jill screamed. Mike kept the pedal to the floor and continued driving back into town with his white knuckles gripping the wheel like a life source.

They made it to a well-lit parking lot at the entryway of Chillicothe. Mike pulled into a parking spot and put it into park. Jill opened the door and leaned out of the vehicle. Nichole exited the vehicle to stretch her legs and catch her breath. "Jill? Are you alright" she asked.

Jill was visibly scared, but she just looked up at Nichole and said, "Now I am." Nick got out of the vehicle and proceeded to walk over to Nichole and Jill's side, but something weird caught his attention and stopped him in his tracks. "What the…?" he said aloud. Nichole looked in his direction and responded, "What is that?" Jill stood up and walked over to where Nichole stood to get a better look.

There were mysterious handprints on the back of the car. The vehicle was covered in dust and dirt; however, the handprints were small, fresh and appeared to belong to a female. They were located in the exact area where the thumping sound was heard by the group. The street lights cast their glow on the rear window. Nick noticed a series of handprints all over the trunk lid and back window.

"Who did that?" he said softly.

Jill grabbed on to Mike's hand and said, "Don't you ever take me anywhere like that again! Whatever was there did not want us there!"

Mike nodded in agreement and replied, "I probably shouldn't have said that thing about her baby. I'm sorry guys." Nichole leaned into Nick; she was shaking and searching for his hand. Without saying another word to one another, they all got back into the vehicle and drove back to Jill's house in complete silence.

Scioto Trail State Park

Scioto Trail State Park is along the far south end of Ross County, Ohio. This area was originally a Native American trail that followed the Scioto River from northern Ohio to the hunting grounds of Kentucky. The trail was later used by settlers who traveled upriver from Portsmouth to Chillicothe, the first capital of Ohio. This heavily wooded area is said to be haunted by the spirits of Native Americans, the ghosts of early settlers and hikers who've wandered off marked trails and died from falling, exposure or from being attacked by wild animals.

One haunted tale in particular that stands out is the story of a park ranger and his family who once lived on the property. They lived in a quaint little cabin on the property. This happened during one of the most brutal winters on record in the area. The two-bedroom cabin had a decently sized living room with the fireplace in the center. This was a great way to keep warm in the kitchen and sitting area. The days started early for Paul, and with the days getting dark earlier, he would make it home cold and exhausted. The days felt longer and longer as Paul started to feel weighed down with his workload and stressed out until it was time for bed. His wife, Melody, was a beautiful woman and a wonderful mother to their two children. Paul had always been a jealous man and believed that every man around wanted Melody and would stop at nothing to get their hands on her. The long hours, freezing environment and irrational paranoia slowly started to get the better of him.

Rolling hills. *Kristin Parks Photography.*

His one beer a week on Fridays turned into one beer at the end of each day. This habit turned into day drinking that led to him lashing out in anger toward anyone he felt didn't show him the respect that he felt he deserved.

"Have a good day today, Paul. Please try," Melody said to Paul as he reached for the door.

He turned to look back at her and offered a halfhearted smile. "I'll do what I can, dear." He pulled the door closed, harder than usual, and stormed off into the frigid darkness to his truck. Melody started to straighten up in the kitchen while her two little ones were still sleeping in their room. Paul started his day on the far end of the park. Coyotes were spotted in the area the day before. He pulled into the parking area near the pond and put the truck in park. Paul decided to sit and watch the sunrise before he started to set traps for the coyotes.

His day drinking started early this morning—vodka was now his breakfast of choice. His head was full of random thoughts of sadness, anger and regret. *Why did I move me and my family out here? I've grown to hate this job. I've grown to hate myself,* he said silently to himself. Melody was making breakfast for the little ones as they were slowly waking from their deep sleep. Before she was able to finish, there was a knock at the door. It had been a few hours since Paul had left. "Who could that be?" Melody said to herself. She went to the door and peeked around the corner to see who it was before opening the door. It was Paul's assistant, Stan. Melody answered the door to greet him. "Morning, ma'am." Stan said to her as the door opened fully. Melody was surprised to see Stan at the house, considering how late it was in the morning.

"Sorry to stop over uninvited, but have you seen Paul? He was supposed to meet me at the north radio tower over an hour ago," Stan said. Melody gave him a puzzled look. She looked over her shoulder at the kids to make sure they weren't aware of the conversation. "I'm sorry, Stan, Paul left very early this morning. He couldn't wait to start his day," Melody said as her eyes scanned the floor. Stan noticed her body language and the look of concern mixed with sadness. He didn't feel that it was his place to pry any further into what goes on behind the doors of other people. Stan replied, "I'm sure it's nothing. He probably just got busy setting coyote traps and forgot to meet me at the tower. I'll find him, don't you worry, ma'am."

Melody smiled and shifted her posture, standing a little bit taller after hearing such reassurances. Her daughter was consumed with curiosity and wandered over to the door to greet their visitor. "Hello, mister!" Angeline said to Stan. Melody looked down at her and placed her hand on her head. Stan chuckled and replied, "Well hello, Miss Angeline. How are you on this fine morning?" She smiled and leaned into her mother's hip, hiding her face. "Oh don't be shy now. You know Mr. Stan. He's a friend." Melody said.

"Mom! There's smoke in the kitchen!" Marcus shouted from the hallway. Melody turned to see fire and black smoke billowing from the stovetop. Stan stepped in and ran over to the fire, removing his overcoat and smothering the flame. Melody was amazed with his quick action to eliminate the threat. She hadn't seen Paul move quickly like that or show that kind of concern for them since before they moved into the cabin. This job had somehow changed him for the worse. "Thank you so much, Stan. You saved us!" Melody said as she moved closer to him and started to hug him. Stan stiffened when she grabbed him. He feared that she may have misread his intentions. Sure, he thought she was kind and beautiful, but he was not making a move on another man's wife.

THE SOUND OF COYOTES startled Paul and pulled him out of his deep sleep. He had apparently fallen asleep waiting for coyotes to show up. A large amount of snow had accumulated during the time that he had passed out drunk while waiting. He scanned the area around him and noticed a large pack of coyotes. "So much for setting traps. No way am I doing that now."

Paul said to himself. He could see his breath as he sat there in the truck. The rear and driver's side windows were fogged up from when Paul was asleep. He checked his watch and realized that he'd been out for a while. "Well, there goes the morning. It's already lunch time." Paul said aloud. He started the truck and revved the engine.

The sound startled the coyotes, and they scattered into the woods. As the grounds near the pond cleared, he noticed something that shook him to the core. He locked eyes with someone who was standing along the tree line. This person looked like him but was covered in blood and looked like he had lost his mind. There was a crazed look in his eyes. Paul grabbed his hidden vodka bottle from under the seat and took a long drink. He rubbed his eyes and looked back at the tree line, but the vision was gone. Shaken by this encounter, Paul started to make his way home for lunch.

Melody and Stan were having coffee as he cleaned the burned area around the stove. "I think that should do it, ma'am. It looks much cleaner now. You can't even tell there was ever a fire," Stan said to Melody. He handed the used dish towels back to Melody so she could deal with them and returned his coffee cup. "Well, ma'am, I need to get back to the station. I hope I can find Paul there." He headed out to his truck and started his journey back to the ranger station in search of Paul.

The weather started to get bad as Paul was heading home for lunch. As he pulled up to the house, he noticed another set of tracks near the house. His drunken mind was filled with angry thoughts and the fire of jealousy. Paul took another long swig of vodka and started the short walk to the front door. Melody was inside preparing lunch for Paul when he burst through the door. "Who is it, Melody? Who is here? Where are they hiding?" he shouted as he swung his arm and ripped several pictures and a shelf from the wall.

Melody backed away and shook with fear. "Paul? What is wrong with you? Have you been drinking?" she said. Paul walked in closer toward her and noticed Stan's heavy overcoat on the chair of the kitchen set. This really angered Paul and caused him to flip the table over.

"What is Stan's coat doing here? What was he doing here, Melody? What were you two doing?" Paul shouted as he grabbed her arm and pulled her closer.

She jerked away from him and responded, "There was a fire and he used his coat to put it out!"

"That don't answer my question! Why was he here?" He pushed her as he asked that question. Melody fell back and slammed the back of her neck into the stovetop. Everything became silent. Her lifeless body fell to the ground. Paul had broken her neck from the impact. Their two little ones ran to their mother's side.

"Momma, wake up! Wake up!" their daughter shouted as she held her face with her tiny hands. Paul had lost his mind at this point. His anger issues and jealousy mixed with alcoholism had finally taken control of him. He took the small round kitchen table, lifted it and slammed it onto Melody's lifeless body. Without even realizing it, he ended the lives of his two children with that one single act. His head started to spin and pound. Paul started to gag and vomit into the kitchen sink and completely passed out.

When Paul regained consciousness, it was completely dark in the house except for the small bulb over the sink. He looked out the window and saw the night sky. He had blacked out from all the drinking and jealous rage. He looked over at the destroyed table and realized that his wife and two children had been killed due to his drunken actions. Paul sat there for a moment and looked at his coat and boots—they had blood spatter on them. The blood of his innocent wife and children stained his clothing and the kitchen floor. He placed his head in his hands and began to sob.

After a few moments, he grabbed on to the counter to pull himself up. He stood shaking, crying and losing his mind over his actions. Paul finally gathered himself, ran water over his hands and splashed his face. He grabbed a new bottle of vodka from the pantry and took three huge swigs. His pounding headache had returned, followed by a ringing in his ear. He beat his fists on the countertop and let out a visceral scream. Paul took a deep breath and looked back at his dead family. He peered out through the kitchen window and focused on the well next to the house.

He knelt down to scoop up his wife's lifeless body and proceeded to walk to the well. Paul lowered her onto the freezing ground and removed the cover from the outer lip of the bricked top layer. Paul stood still and gazed aimlessly into the well. He looked around the wooded area and then back at the house. Paul took a deep breath, picked up Melody one last time and then dropped her into the well. After he heard the echo and a splash, he stepped back and looked into the sky. He could see his breath as a light snow started to fall. Paul repeated the same process two more times as he disposed of the bodies of his children.

Once he was finished, he sauntered back into the cabin, slammed the door and then finished the bottle of vodka. He made his way to the wall where his shotgun was mounted. After checking the gun for ammo, he noticed that it was loaded. Paul quickly positioned the gun under his chin, aiming toward the back of his head. Stretching with all his strength, he pulled the trigger and turned the lights out permanently. Since that horrible night, there have been several stories that revolve around that cabin. Rangers and their families who moved in and out of that cabin have all had experiences with phantom sounds, shadows, cries and screams. The cabin no longer stands where it once did. The years passed by, and the house became vacant. Then it was destroyed by fire. The well where the bodies were said to have been dumped is now covered and hidden in a little barn that was built around it. When you travel through Scioto Trail State Park, you can see the barn from the road on your way to the campgrounds. Hikers, bicyclists, campers and locals have reported that you can hear cries and screams coming from this property. If you're ever in the area, visit this site and see for yourself.

Paranormal Encounters at the Majestic Theatre

The official website for the Majestic Theatre tells us that this location claims to be "America's oldest continuously operating theater." The theater opened in 1853 as the Masonic Hall and began showing motion pictures with the state-of-the-art Edison Vitascope in 1896. Since then, the theater has exhibited films and live performances ranging from operas to vaudeville acts. Today, the Majestic operates as a nonprofit and hosts community events, live performances and movie nights. The Majestic Theatre started out as the Masonic Hall, built in 1853. After the building was enlarged in 1876, it became known as the Masonic Opera House and was considered one of the finest theaters in Ohio.

In 1895, the opera house was equipped with electric lights, making it one of the first buildings in Chillicothe with electricity. In fact, the building even sold electricity from its generator to parts of the city. One year later, the theater began showing motion pictures with the Edison Vitascope, making it the first movie theater in town. In 1904, a man named A.R. Wolf bought the Masonic Opera House and remodeled it. He enlarged the stage and added permanent seats and stained-glass windows. In 1907, Wolf constructed an arch across Second Street to add to the grandeur. It still stands today. Wolf sold the theater to the Myers brothers in 1915. They were the owners who changed the theater's name to the Majestic and who chose the exhibition of movies over live performances. Still, there was the occasional vaudeville performance

The show must go on. *Neal Parks Photography*.

over the years. Of the top one hundred performers of the time, the Majestic hosted at least eighty-eight at various points. The brothers also added the words *Vaudeville* and *Majestic* in neon lights to the arch in 1918 (*Vaudeville* was later removed). That same year, Chillicothe was dealing with the Spanish influenza pandemic. Hundreds of soldiers died at the nearby Camp Sherman, and their bodies were brought to the Lowery Mortuary across the street from the Majestic.

When the mortuary became overcrowded, bodies were stored in the dressing rooms, under the stage and the downstairs hall of the theater and even embalmed on stage. The bodily fluids from this process were tossed into the alley by the theater, thus giving this location the nickname "Blood Alley." The Majestic Theatre was restored in the 1970s after being purchased by Harley and Evelyn Bennet. New seats and doors were installed while the restrooms and lobby were updated. The roof and marquee were also refurbished. In 1990, three local businessmen— Robert Althoff, Robert Evans and David Uhrig—bought the theater as a nonprofit organization. Today, the Majestic Theatre hosts live performances, community events and classic movie nights. Visitors can also request a tour of the historic theater.

There is no shortage of ghost stories and paranormal encounters when it comes to this haunted hot spot. I have had several experiences during my visits to the theater while conducting research and when attending shows. I have also collected hundreds upon hundreds of different ghost stories and eyewitness accounts from so many people through the years. After a lot of reading and piecing together the best stories shared with me and one that I experienced, I narrowed it down to a few creepy tales to share. My hope is that the few stories that you are about to read will inform, entertain and scare you.

The Usher

In the dimly lit corridors of the Majestic Theatre, many people have reported speaking with, seeing and hearing a spectral figure known as the Ghost Usher. Legend has it that he was a devoted usher in his earthly life, ensuring that patrons found their seats with a smile. However, the story goes that a tragedy struck when he met an untimely end during a backstage accident. Now, as a ghostly presence, the Usher continues his duties, guiding unseen audiences to their seats during performances. Some say that they feel a cool breeze and hear faint echoes of polite whispers as he assists them to their places.

Despite his ethereal form, the Ghost Usher is said to have a keen eye for theater etiquette. Actors and crew members swear that they've felt his unseen hand straightening costumes or adjusting props, always striving for perfection in the performances he once loved. As the final curtain falls, the ghostly figure is rumored to stand near the exit, nodding in approval at the applause. The Majestic Theatre has embraced its spectral usher, considering him a guardian of the arts, forever haunting the hallowed halls in service to the magic of the stage.

A Night at the Theater

Maggie and Katey were excited for their mother-and-daughter movie night at the Majestic. It was a special holiday feature of *It's a Wonderful Life*. They were ready with advance tickets in their hands. On their journey, though, they were surprised by a sudden snowstorm. They didn't live far from the theater, but it felt like the longest drive of their lives. Upon arriving at the Majestic, they figured that the likelihood of finding a worthwhile parking spot was slim.

Luckily, there was an open space after all, and they safely parked and took the short walk into the theater. The lobby was bustling with beautiful Christmas decorations and the smell of pine, popcorn and coffee. People were moving in all directions from the lobby to their seats, both upstairs and along the main floor. "There are so many people here already, Mom!" Katey said.

Maggie looked around and then read their tickets. "Fortunately, we won't have to climb all of those stairs. Our seats are on the first floor."

A well-dressed usher stepped out from behind the main doors leading to the seating area. He extended his hand, nodded his head and motioned them toward the entrance. "How cool! Look, Mom, they're dressed in an old-fashioned usher uniform!" Katey said aloud.

Maggie smiled and responded, "That is so cool. They're really getting in the spirit for this presentation." The usher led them to their seats as they followed close behind him. Maggie was digging through her purse for a tip to give to this helpful usher.

Maggie took her seat first, and Katey followed behind her. "Here, Katey, hand this to him please." Katey took the money and turned to hand it to the usher, but he was nowhere to be found. It was as if he had vanished into thin air.

"Mom! Uhh, he's, he's gone. He was standing right next to me, then he wasn't." Maggie leaned forward and noticed that the usher was gone. She turned to look around where they had walked from and didn't see the usher anywhere. Katey took her seat and grabbed her mother's hand. "Who was that, Mom? Are we losing our minds?" Katey asked.

Maggie replied, "No, dear. We both saw him and spoke to him, he was there." She suddenly realized that he never responded to them—he just walked ahead of them and motioned with his hands.

During intermission, Katey got up to grab a drink at the concession stand. Maggie stood in the lobby and waited. She continued to scan the crowd in search of the usher who had led them to their seats. An employee was walking past them as they were getting ready to go back in. "Excuse me, miss. I have a question. Do you have ushers in formal attire working today?" Maggie asked.

The theater employee looked puzzled by the question. She looked at Katey and then back at Maggie. She responded, "We haven't had ushers in this theater since the early 1960s." Katey grabbed tightly to her mother's hand and looked at her. Maggie thanked the employee for the information and then looked at Katey. She said, "Well, Katey, let's go back to our seats on our own."

THE GIRL IN THE BASEMENT

The Majestic Theatre is known for many things. Legends tell of whispers echoing over the years about a ghostly presence residing in the basement and dressing room area. The stories are all the same. They normally involve a young girl known as Abigail, who met a tragic end within these very halls. Abigail was the daughter of an actress who would travel from city to city for her performances. She had an ethereal charm that enchanted all those who encountered her. Her love for the stage knew no bounds. However, her love of the stage and the fame wove a cruel thread when, one fateful night, a fire started in the hotel next to the theater after an amazing performance.

As the chaos engulfed the top floors, Abigail was running to the lobby in an attempt to escape. Her mother had vanished amid the panic. The front doors were locked from the inside, and the keys were nowhere to be found. She noticed that the access to the basement of the hotel was left open. Abigail ran down the stairs to see if the underground connector between the Majestic and the hotel was open. Unfortunately, there was a fire in the basement as well. She was blinded by the smoke as she pushed open the exit to the connector. The smoke followed as she ran to the end of the hall. Abigail attempted to push open the doors to the Majestic, but they were also locked.

Within just a few moments, the hall was full of black smoke. Her efforts proved futile. Abigail succumbed to smoke inhalation and died by the door of the Majestic's basement. Many have claimed to have heard her laughter echoing in the dressing rooms and along the walkways, or they've glimpsed her ghostly figure dancing in the darkness. There have been many theater participants who have shared stories of their encounter with the young spirit that haunts the basement and dressing rooms. An actress whom I will call Molly was getting ready for the premiere of a musical she was in and saw the ghost girl in her dressing room.

Molly felt the presence of someone else in the room with her. She had been alone for a short while, going over her lines as she was getting dressed. She turned to look over her shoulder, but there was nothing there. She then turned to look at herself in the mirror to touch up her hair and makeup. Her heart dropped when she noticed a little girl standing directly behind her. Molly jumped up out of her seat and ran for the door. She turned to look back into the dressing room only to realize that there was no one else in the room with her. Molly stood in the doorway, dumbfounded and speechless. She slowly stepped back, away from the room, and noticed the little girl out of the corner of her eye as the ghostly figure skipped down the hall and disappeared near the door of the basement.

THE JANITOR IS WATCHING

My personal encounter—which was chronicled on Fox28 News and relayed in my first book, *Paranormal Chronicles: Tales of Humor, Horror and the Absolutely Strange*—dealt with an entity that appeared before me. This encounter has remained permanently etched in my mind, and I have shared this story countless times. It was October 1995, during a showing of a few classic B horror films. During the first intermission, I walked through the lobby, passed a few other people who were enjoying themselves and headed toward the restroom area.

The steps that led to the basement level went through a narrow hall that had a shorter ceiling than the height of an average person. The restrooms were immediately to the left at the bottom step of the basement level. I was the only person down there at the time, and the feeling left me with a sense of paranoia. The ghost stories that I had heard about this place put me in a panicky state of mind. I quickly shrugged it off as just an overactive imagination and continued with what I was doing. I walked into the men's room and almost jumped out of the costume I was wearing when I spotted a janitor mopping the floor to the right of me. I laughed to myself after realizing that a janitor with a mop and bucket was the least of my worries.

"Whoa, sorry about that, sir. I almost ran right into you," I said to the janitor. He continued to mop like he was shackled to the task, without so much as a glance after my apologetic greeting. After a few minutes, the silence remained, and I proceeded to wash my hands. I noticed that the janitor was in the same spot continuing to mop the same area without stopping. I attempted to strike up a conversation with him once more while I washed my hands.

"That must be the cleanest spot in this entire bathroom," I said to the janitor. He stopped what he was doing and looked up at me. His stare was vacant and lifeless. I felt an instant blast of cold as he looked intently right through me. I was thankful that I had already used the restroom at that point. I was fear-stricken upon noticing that he had been mopping the floor this entire time without a bucket present; however, the floor was soaked and glistened as brightly as a Mop & Glo advertisement. The janitor turned quickly and exited through the door to the right. I couldn't move at first. I felt as if my legs each weighed a ton. I forced myself to move forward so I could see where he was headed and who he really was. I rushed back upstairs, but the janitor was nowhere to be seen on the staircase or in the lobby.

I stood next to the concession stand for what felt like minutes before I realized that someone from somewhere was watching me. There were several people in the lobby, and another movie was starting. I felt alone even though others surrounded me. I felt an unsettling urge to look upward. There he was, like a vulture perched above its prey—the janitor was directly above me, at the edge of the second-floor balcony railing, staring at me as if he wanted me to leave. I continued to observe him and watch his movements with the utmost wariness. He quickly turned as sporadically as he did before.

I couldn't help myself. I started up the stairway to the second floor. The janitor watched me as I made it three steps to the top and watched him turn and walk down the walkway near the balcony entrance and then directly to a door at the end of that hall. He walked *through* the physical door, without even turning the doorknob. The janitor simply vanished into the door as if he had been swallowed up by some black hole. I quickly walked down the same hall and grabbed the doorknob for the room. Upon opening the door, it was revealed to be a janitor's closet with cleaning supplies and boxes in storage. I slowly backed away from the room, closed the door and noticed that there were dozens of pictures lining the wall along the hall. One of the pictures was a cast and crew picture from the early 1950s. The same janitor I had encountered and followed until he disappeared was in that picture. He was wearing the same work uniform and the same hairstyle. This has been an encounter that I've shared on my podcast, in an earlier book, to groups of schoolchildren and at book signings. Hopefully the story will age as well as the Majestic Theatre itself.

HIGBY HOUSE

DREAM HOME FOR SALE

This Greek Revival home built in 1857 goes by the name Higby House. It is also known as Dresbach House and has many stories of strange encounters and ghostly tales that surround it. One such story pertains to a family who were considering purchasing the home since they first visited during an open house. They fell in love with the home as they went from room to room, taking in all of its architectural beauty. Their daughter was enamored of the downstairs area thanks to the children's playroom area, couch, TV, pool table and shag carpeting. As they explored that level of the home, they felt a strange energy there, as if they were being watched and followed by something or someone.

"So, have you fallen in love with this cozy home?" the real estate agent asked as she descended the stairs. The family had their attention pulled from the ominous feeling that they had been experiencing.

The matriarch of the family replied, "Yes! Uh, yes of course. We love this place. Have there been any offers made yet?"

The agent's face lit up with anticipation. "There have not been any offers made yet. I can put one in for you if you would like," she responded with high hopes. She joined them and continued to show them around the basement bedroom, bathroom and exercise room.

Their small daughter asked the agent, "What's in that room?" The agent looked in the direction of the door she was pointing at. She slowly walked toward the area and stopped abruptly. Something felt off as she approached

Higby House. *Don O'Brien*.

the door and started to open it. "Who's that little girl mommy?" their daughter asked. Everyone present looked at one another, confused by what the young girl had just said.

"I'm sorry, honey. What little girl are you talking about?" the agent asked.

The little girl pointed at the door and said, "She was at the top of the staircase when we came in. She's following us all around." Her parents placed their hands on their daughter in an attempt to silence her. The real estate agent lost all of the color in her face as she looked in the area where the little girl was pointing. She noticed another little girl with pigtails, wearing a white dress.

"Who is that?" the agent asked. Everyone else in the room turned to look in the same direction and saw the same little girl as she slowly vanished into the wall behind her.

The real estate agent and the little girl's parents ran toward the stairs. The little girl remained downstairs, walking down the hall to where the little girl had disappeared. She opened the door to the room and slowly walked in.

The room was dark and empty. Meanwhile, upstairs, her parents realized that their daughter was not with them.

"Mike! Where's April?" Sarah asked. Mike looked behind him and then ran toward the doorway to the basement stairs.

"Oh my God! April! April!" Mike shouted. The agent, Mike and Sarah started downstairs in search of her. They were running toward the back hall where they saw the little girl vanish. April was in that room. The door slammed shut, locking her in the dark room.

"Mommy! Mommy! I can't see! Daddy!" April screamed to them as she pounded on the door.

Her parents grabbed the doorknob and pushed hard against the door. "The door won't budge!" Mike said. "Push harder! Push harder!" Sarah cried out. They could hear a child giggling and singing, coming from inside the room. They let go of the door, and it slowly opened by itself. They rushed inside and saw their daughter sitting on the floor, facing the wall and giggling as the sound of another little girl's singing filled the air. They placed their hands on April, and she shook as she looked up at them.

"Mommy! Daddy! There's a little girl named Laura stuck in this house. A mean older woman named Nancy keeps her here and won't let her go to heaven, where her mommy and daddy live. She slammed the door on me, and Laura helped me."

Her parents looked at each other with pale faces and mouths open. They looked at the real estate agent and said, "This is not the house for us. We are not putting an offer on this place." They took their daughter and quickly walked up the stairs and out of the house. They did not end up buying the home.

The Nightmare Mansion

A former resident of the Higby House shared this next story. He came face to face with a ghostly little girl at the top of the stairs while living there in the early 1990s. Tim purchased the property with the hopes of flipping the house and starting a family. He was in his mid-twenties with big dreams and a solid job with the city department. After a few days of working on the house during a long weekend, he decided that he was going to spend his first night in his new home and get better acquainted with the land and surrounding environment. Tim had just finished stripping and cleaning the floor in the living room and kitchen before realizing that it was already 12:52 a.m. He was beyond exhausted and decided to stop where he was and collect as much trash as he physically could before passing out. Tim slowly climbed to the top of the stairs and fell into his bed. Without a care in the world, he fell fast asleep. The sound of footsteps was soon heard coming from down the hall. The uninvited noise woke Tim abruptly. He sat up a little to check the time—3:10 a.m. *What is that?* he thought to himself. The sound of footsteps continued as Tim listened closely for the source. The sound continued and appeared to get closer. Tim sat all the way up in bed and leaned over to look down the hall. The moonlight shined through and cast a light along the walls. He could see the outline of someone near the doorway to his room. *What the…?* Tim thought to himself. Now, completely awake and getting out of bed to stand up, he shouted aloud, "Hey! Who are you!"

He reached over to turn on the light in the room and grabbed a steel pipe that was on the floor near him. "You better have a good reason for being here!" Tim said as he stomped toward the doorway. As he got closer, he noticed that the outline of the intruder had disappeared. He turned on the hall light and stood for a while, just listening and watching. Tim took a walk around the house and checked all of the rooms, windows and doors. Everything was locked, and all the rooms were empty. He felt that the whole encounter was just his exhaustion playing tricks on him. Tim went back to bed but left the light on with his door cracked. Some time passed, and he was once again woken abruptly. Tim experienced the feeling of being held down by something while in bed, and the entire room was cold and completely dark. He struggled to move and found it hard to breathe. Something heavy was on him, but he couldn't see anything or anyone else in the room. Tim started to panic and was overexerting himself to break free. He cried out, "Get off me! Who are you? Get off of me now!"

After Tim said that, his bedroom door flung open, and the hall light started to turn off and on. Tim was finally able to sit up. He ran from the room and down the stairs. He grabbed his truck keys and wasted no time as he headed out of the house and ran without shoes through the snow to his vehicle. Tim looked up at the window to his room and saw a little girl with pigtails peering out from the window, smiling at him. He started his truck and destroyed part of the yard trying to leave the property. He never returned to the house and sold it as is to another interested buyer.

THE GIRL OF THE HOUSE

Mike lived there in the early 1990s. The Higby House had sat empty for close to eight years before his family moved in. He was only in the sixth grade and was no older than twelve. His parents were renting the home from the Dreshach family at the time. He remembers seeing the house for the first time and thinking to himself, as any child with an overactive imagination would, *This house has ghosts.* Little did he know how true his thoughts would turn out to be. The first encounter he had with the "prior inhabitants" of the home actually happened in the middle of the day. He was having an argument with his mother in the kitchen. They went back and forth a couple of times, and Mike was instructed to go to his room until dinner. "Fine! I'll go there and stare out the window!" he said to his mother as he stormed off to his room.

As Mike started the climb to the top of the spiral staircase, he froze in his tracks. There before him was a young girl, maybe no more than seven years old. She was wearing dingy, turn-of-the-century, *Little House on the Prairie*–style clothing. "Hi. Uh, hello?" Mike said to her. The little girl's eyes were there, but they were not. They seemed to be black, with no signs of life in them. This encounter felt like an eternity but lasted no more than a few seconds. When he finally managed to muster the courage to move toward her, she turned around and walked into the next room. That room used to be the old maid's quarters. During their time there, it had always been abandoned. The little girl disappeared into that room.

Mike's family was not a wealthy family, which was why they were renting the home. During their time at the Higby House, Mike shared a bedroom and bed with his younger brother. After his meeting with the little girl, he became terrified of the home and, more specifically, with the home at night. He was given a night light that he kept plugged into the wall at the foot of his bed, just for the extra bit of security. Mike awoke one night feeling as if he were being held down by something. He could not move. He could not talk. He could not even scream. All visible light in the room was gone.

The only thing Mike could see was total darkness. He was beyond petrified, and as quickly as it had woken him, it was gone. "Mom! Dad! Help!" Mike cried out when he was finally able to. During this whole encounter, his brother was next to him, sleeping like the dead. Mike was not able to see him or his night light. His parents rushed in to see what was wrong after hearing the cries for help.

"What in the world is wrong? You're screaming like the place is on fire!" Mike's father said. When they entered the room, Mike's mother screamed after seeing a strange-looking little girl standing in the corner of the room. His dad looked at the same corner where his wife was staring and also noticed the little girl. "Hey! Who are you? You don't belong here!" Mike's father said. Everything in the room grew eerily silent as the little girl moved suddenly and floated toward Mike's parents. His dad fell backward as she got closer to them. The little girl ran through his mother and vanished down the hall. Mike and his family grabbed what they could and ran out of the house to their van. They drove to his grandparents' house and spent the night. Mike and his family returned a few days later during the daylight hours and retrieved their belongings. That was the last time they ever slept in that home.

GRANDVIEW CEMETERY

This cemetery is located in Chillicothe, Ohio, at the end of Brookside Drive, which is the entrance road into the cemetery. The ninety-two-acre Grandview Cemetery was established around 1841. The cemetery contains the graves of four important Ohio governors, a famous Civil War general and pioneer founders of Ohio. Its monuments are of superior workmanship and feature detailing in the Gothic Revival, Greek Revival, Romanesque and early twentieth-century Classical Revival styles. There are countless stories of shadowy figures that have been seen strolling through the cemetery late at night. Tales of strange mists near the mausoleums have been seen by people, and many have felt as if they are being watched.

CHASING SHADOWS

A few friends ventured out to the cemetery late one night and were exploring the area. They were gathering around an obelisk and waiting for another one of their friends. They saw him about two hundred yards away, walking perpendicular to where they were facing. He was silhouetted against the night sky and was strolling slowly. One of the friends said, "Hey, there's Daniel! He made it." A few seconds passed after they said

Gateway. *Neal Parks Photography.*

that, and then the real Daniel came walking up to them from a completely different direction. He wasn't even in their peripheral vision from where they had spotted the figure.

The group of friends went to where they had seen the shadowy figure, but it had walked into the woods by then. "I swear that looked like Daniel!" Jennifer said.

"I know for a fact it wasn't me." Daniel replied. They decided to reenact him walking up the same path to see if perhaps it was some freak occurrence involving a spooky shadow. Mike watched from the same spot along with Jennifer, Luke and Heather. Daniel's attempt didn't replicate what they had seen earlier. Daniel stopped moving and stood there, looking up at them. "Who is that over there?" Daniel shouted to the others. They looked over in the area where he was staring and saw a man, holding a rifle over his shoulder and dressed in a Civil War uniform. He was standing next to a tall tombstone with a cross etched in it.

They're watching. *Neal Parks Photography*.

When the group saw how close he was to all of them, they panicked and ran down the hill toward Daniel. "Come on, Daniel! We are getting out of here! This is nuts!" Mike said as they stampeded their way out of the cemetery and to their vehicle. They saw another person near the exit as they sped away. It looked like an older woman in a long white gown. She was semi-transparent and smiled menacingly at the group of friends. This caused Mike to drive even faster, leaving their phantoms behind them covered in a trail of dust.

Capture the Flag

Todd and his friends were hanging around at the cemetery one evening to get a clear view of the sunset. This is one of the reasons it's referred to as "the Grandview." They were playing capture the flag earlier and exploring the area. It is a very large cemetery, and there is a lot to see when visiting. The group of friends were joking back and forth about school, home and where they might be in five years. "I bet you'll end up being the mayor of Chillicothe, Todd!" one of the guys from the group said jokingly.

Todd laughed and replied, "I would end up bankrupting the city!" They all agreed and continued to wait for the sun to set. A strange noise could be heard close to where they were standing.

"Did anyone else hear that?" Steve asked. Everyone got really quiet and listened closely. The sound was heard again, this time by everyone. It sounded closer at this point and caused everyone to look at the mausoleum.

"Is that the door to that tomb slamming over and over?" Todd inquired. The group slowly made their way toward the area.

Steve spoke up, "Guys! Those doors keep slamming on their own!"

Todd responded, "Could someone be trapped in there?" The doors flung open, exposing the total darkness inside the mausoleum. Todd put his arm out in an attempt to stop the group from moving forward.

"What do we do Todd? Is someone in there?" Mark asked. Steve knelt down and picked up a rock, tossing it into the darkness. The group of friends shuddered in fear as the sound of the rock could be heard bouncing from the floor to the wall and then back to the floor. It grew silent as the group stood, waiting for someone to make another move. A strange sigh, followed with a heavy breath, could be heard coming from the darkness.

Resting. *Neal Parks Photography*.

Everyone in attendance stood and looked at one another and then looked back into the blackened tomb.

"Is anyone in there?" Todd asked. A few seconds went by before a thundering growl came pouring out from inside, followed by the gravely words, "Get out!" A cold blast of air shot out, hitting the group of friends and chilling them to their core. The group turned away and ran back to their vehicles. As the sun finished setting on the cemetery grounds, the grand view could be seen in their rearview mirrors as they sped away.

The Lady in Mourning

In the moonlit silence of Grandview Cemetery, stories are told of shadows weaving through weathered tombstones. Legends whisper of a spectral figure, the Lady in Mourning, who roams among the graves, searching for a lost love. Locals speak of eerie wails echoing through the night—the ghostly lament of a broken heart. Visitors claim to see flickering lights and ethereal orbs dancing near the historic mausoleum, where restless spirits are said to linger. Some share tales of encountering cold spots and hearing faint whispers that send shivers down their spines.

One warm evening, a daring group ventured into the cemetery armed with flashlights and skepticism. As the clock struck midnight, a ghostly apparition materialized, veiled in sorrow. The air grew heavy with an otherworldly presence, and the temperature around the small group of friends plummeted. The Lady in Mourning beckoned, her solemn gaze fixed on a forgotten grave.

"Why is she looking at that grave? She's totally pointing at it!" Lucas said. The ghost moved closer to the tombstone and knelt down in front of it.

"What is she doing?" Riley asked. Desperate for closure, the Lady stood up and moved along the path. She turned and looked at the group, motioning for them to follow her. She led the group to a weathered headstone.

Beneath the moon's glow, they noticed that the tombstone was covered in moss and vines. It was an older tombstone, much like the one where the Lady had been kneeling. Lucas, Steven and Hendrix started to pull away the vines and used a flat rock to scrape away the moss and years of grime. Riley held the flashlight while Molly and Ellie read the inscription on the headstone: "Mr Thomas Woods, Loving Father and Husband to Ruby, Born 1834–1928," Ellie read aloud.

Telling no tales. *Neal Parks Photography*.

Lucas realized that Ruby must've been the name of the Lady in Mourning. "That must be her tombstone that she was kneeling by. Why isn't she buried next to her husband?" Lucas asked. They went back to the first stone in order to read it.

Hendrix asked Riley for the flashlight so they could read it. "Look at that! Her name was Ruby. You were right, Lucas," Hendrix said.

Ellie and Riley read the inscription aloud. "Here lies Mrs Ruby Woods, Loving Wife and Mother Born 1839–1918. Taken too soon by the Spanish Flu." Molly and Hendrix stood beside each other, fixated on the headstone. "Oh my God. She died before her husband from the flu outbreak of 1918," Hendrix said. "She died before her husband. How did he end up buried over there?" Molly added. The phantom woman was then seen by the group kneeling in front of her long-lost husband's grave. She placed her hand on the headstone and ran her fingers across his etched name. "That's really weird. What is she looking for?" Lucas said.

The spirit of her husband then appeared standing next to his tombstone. He looked down at her and extended his hand. He helped to bring her up to his level. The two of them embraced and looked into each other's eyes. Riley grabbed Lucas's hand and said, "After all these years, they finally found each other." Since that night, the Lady in Mourning is said to have found solace, her spirit finally at rest. Yet Grandview Cemetery remains a haunting reminder of the thin veil between the living and the departed, where the echoes of the past linger in the midnight air.

HOPEWELL CULTURE NATIONAL HISTORICAL PARK

The Hopewell Culture National Historical Park, also known as Mound City, is a local paranormal hot spot in Chillicothe, Ohio, that sits along State Route 104/Veterans Parkway. This is an area that has a long history of UFO sightings, encounters with strange cryptids and ghostly apparitions. The site is said to be haunted by the mound builders, who originally constructed the earthworks there. It is also supposed to be haunted by the soldiers from Camp Sherman, who leveled the mounds and later died from the Spanish flu after returning home after the First World War.

Many people believe that the reason Camp Sherman was ground zero for the pandemic in the Midwest was a direct result of what the U.S. military had done to this sacred site. Hundreds of locals, tourists and employees both former and current have all shared stories of experiences with the unknown in and around this Hopewell site. Stories of strange sounds, balls of light, shadows and phantom smells have become a common occurrence at this location. A former employee of this historical park shared a strange story with me about an encounter they had while working late one evening.

The park had closed a few hours earlier, and Melody was finishing up an inventory in the gift shop and placing orders for office supplies. She was reviewing some of the live footage from the security cameras and switching camera feeds. "Who is that? We've been closed for over two hours now," she said to herself as she zoomed in with the camera toggle to get a better look at this mystery person. She couldn't believe her eyes! The individual she was looking at was dressed in the same World War I garb that was on display

Welcome. Enjoy. *Neal Parks Photography*.

in their museum. She got up from her office chair to check on the museum displays to see if any of the uniforms were missing.

To her surprise, everything was still in place—nothing had been removed or disturbed. "Where did that uniform come from?" Melody said aloud. She walked quickly back to the monitor station to get a better look at this person. She panned the area where she had first seen this person, but they were no longer there. Melody moved the camera back to the left, then to the right—the person she saw was simply gone. The encounter left her a little unnerved, but she tried to push it aside so she could finish her work for the day. She gathered some of the smaller boxes and a wastepaper basket and made her way toward the back of the office.

When Melody opened the rear door, she placed a small brick at the bottom of the door as she always did. This prevented it from closing behind you on the way to the dumpster. With boxes and trash in her hands, Melody froze in her tracks after locking eyes with the same person she saw earlier on surveillance. The person of interest was perfectly dressed in a World War I uniform, with a gun over his shoulder. He stood silently, staring at Melody, and then looked to his left. Without saying a word, the mystery person turned and quickly walked in the direction he was looking. He walked with a sense of urgency and then completely vanished before her eyes.

Melody dropped everything in her hands, ran back to the rear door, kicked the brick out of the way and pulled the door shut hard. She didn't notice that she had held her breath the entire time she was running back to the office. Melody felt very lightheaded as she took her seat at the monitor station. She couldn't believe what she had just experienced. She was overcome with a sense of paranoia that she couldn't shake. She grabbed the computer mouse and started to look through the different camera options from one monitor to another.

What she saw next pulled the breath from her lungs. In the open field, between two of the largest mounds, more than ten people, dressed in World War I uniforms, could be seen walking in the same direction, almost as if they were marching in step. Melody moved quickly to grab her belongings but was too afraid to run outside to her vehicle. Melody quickly walked to her office, shut the door and locked it. Then she sat on the floor against the door to plan her next move. Seeing as how she was too scared to look out the window or even leave the building, she continued to sit until she felt too tired. Melody rolled her coat into a pillow, curled into the fetal position and slept until the sun rose. She awoke to golden warmth casting upon her face. "Thank God! It's daylight!" Melody said to herself.

She grabbed her items and quickly stood up with an exit plan in mind. She opened her office door, looked across the field and checked the monitors. The strangers were no longer there. Melody set the security system and couldn't make it to her car fast enough, fumbling for her keys between running and looking over her shoulder. After Melody slammed her car door and started the vehicle, she drove along the narrow road to the exit, which passes by the same field between the mounds. The men in uniform were no longer visible. Near the exit, she saw the same man in uniform standing along the tree line, just watching her as she drove away. That was the last time Melody worked alone after hours.

THE MOUND BUILDERS

Over the years, many visitors have recounted eerie occurrences with whispers in the wind and shadowy figures sighted along the tree lines and near the mounds. Many have claimed to feel a spectral presence, especially

Hopewell Home. *Isabella Parks Photography*.

during guided tours and small walkthroughs. One moonlit evening, a group of adventurous friends decided to explore the area after dark. Armed with flashlights and nervous laughter, they wandered the silent paths and sacred sites, their voices echoing against the trees and mounds. "Shhh! Guys not too loud! Who knows who can hear us," one of them said as they stayed low on their journey.

As they approached the largest mound, a faint glow emanated from the shadows. Startled, they froze, watching as a figure emerged—an ethereal silhouette, draped in Native American garb. The ghostly form raised its hand, beckoning them closer. "Oh my God! This can't be real!" one of the friends said to the rest of the group. Heartbeats thundered in their chests as they hesitantly obeyed the silent summons. With each step, the figure became more distinct, its face bearing an uncanny resemblance to the long-deceased builders of the mounds that surrounded them. "Guys! He looks just like the pictures of the Hopewell people from inside the museum!" one of them said aloud.

The ghostly presence spoke, its voice echoing through the deserted historical park. The group of friends couldn't understand what the spirit was saying to them. He was speaking in his Native tongue, which both confused and frightened them. Terrified, they fled the mound area. They never returned, but whispers still persist that a ghostly presence is said to continue to roam Mound City, forever enacting his final guard of this sacred site in the afterlife.

PEOPLE OF THE SHADOWS

In the outskirts of Chillicothe, Ohio, beneath the cloak of night, a veil of shadows descended on the sacred Indian mounds. As the moon cast an eerie glow, the air became charged with an otherworldly energy. Those who dared to approach the ancient grounds were met with silent watchers, shadow beings that emerged to enforce an age-old decree. Local folklore spoke of the spectral guardians that patrolled the mounds, ensuring that the sacred land remained undisturbed. Tales warned of mysterious encounters, chilling whispers and shadowy figures that materialized after sunset. The community, respecting the unspoken boundaries, refrained from venturing near the mounds after dark.

Amid the cautious whispers, a group of friends, drawn by the lure of curiosity and skepticism, decided to challenge the supernatural tales. Ignoring the warnings, they embarked on a moonlit escapade to the heart of the ancient site. As they approached, the shadows stirred, coalescing into ominous figures that silently signaled their disapproval. In the dim light, the shadow beings took on an ethereal form, their voices echoing warnings through the night. In a strange tongue, they murmured in unison, a spectral chorus resonating through the air. Undeterred, the group continued their intrusion, dismissing the warnings as mere folklore.

As the trespassers reached the heart of the mounds, the shadows intensified, their forms becoming more defined and threatening. In a chilling display, they projected visions of the land's sacred history to the group, revealing the reverence it once held for Indigenous tribes. The air thickened with a sense of foreboding as the shadows sought to impart a lesson in respect. Suddenly, the ground trembled beneath them and a voice echoed from the shadows, recounting tales of ancient agreements between the land and its original stewards. The intruders, now gripped by fear, hastily retreated as the shadow beings reclaimed their watchful positions.

From that night forward, the warning persisted, carried by those who had glimpsed the spectral enforcers. Chillicothe's Indian mounds remain to this day, a sacred domain guarded by the shadows, reminding all who approach after dark that the land belonged to the spirits of its original caretakers.

Buzzard's Roost

Located outside Chillicothe, Ohio, this 1,300-acre nature preserve has two overlooks that many locals and traveling nature enthusiasts consider to be the best in all of Ohio. Across this rugged landscape, with its highest point reaching over 600 feet above its lowest point, some of the best landscapes in the state can be witnessed. Buzzard's Roost borders the Paint Creek region and offers an amazing view of the gorge near the South Point Lookout Trail. There have been many stories of a ghostly presence said to roam the moonlit woods. Tales of a spectral wolf with eyes that gleam like silver orbs have swept this area. Locals speak of eerie howls echoing through the night, a haunting melody that has sent shivers down the spines of all who've heard it.

Legend has it that the wolf was once a guardian spirit. The wolf protected the ancient forests that surrounded Chillicothe. However, after the turn of the twentieth century, the decimation of many sacred sites left the creature trapped between worlds. The essence of the wolf spirit forever lingered in the ethereal realm. As the town grappled with sightings and whispered tales, a curious teenager named Alex became drawn to the mystery. Armed with a barely bright flashlight and an insatiable curiosity, Alex ventured into the heart of the haunted woods, guided by the soft glow of the moon above, a hiking stick and his flashlight.

The ghost wolf was watching Alex for a while. Drawn to his pure intentions, it revealed itself and stood before Alex in the middle of the trail. Through what would best be described as a silent connection, memories

The descent. *Kristin Parks Photography*.

unfolded—the wolf's once vibrant existence, its kinship with the land and the sorrowful event that bound it to the spirit realm. Determined to help the ghost wolf find peace, Alex delved into Chillicothe's history, uncovering forgotten stories and ancient sites that excavation destroyed. Alex went back to Buzzard's Roost, hoping to encounter the wolf spirit in an attempt to figure out how he might free him. Alex found a huge tree along the trail and sat beneath it to wait for the wolf to appear again.

As Alex waited, he started to doze off and leaned against the tree. Within a few moments, he was out. He started having lucid dreams involving ancient tribes and mound builders, the industrial age ravaging the land and the wolf spirit getting lost in our world after a sacred site was destroyed. Alex jerked awake from the sounds of snarling coyotes surrounding him. He lifted his flashlight to get a better look at what was around him. It was as bad as it sounded—there were four coyotes near him. They looked dangerous and hungry. Alex reached for his hiking stick, prepared for the fight of his life. One of the beasts lunged forward as Alex prepared to swing. An unseen force struck the coyote as it was airborne, knocking it against a tree. The other coyotes noticed something that Alex didn't see. One of them charged toward the middle of the trail and was picked up, shaken hard to the left, then the right, and then slammed hard to the ground.

The remaining coyotes retreated after the invisible force revealed itself. The ghost wolf appeared right when Alex needed it most. He noticed that the first coyote that was taken down had not moved since being thrown into the tree. There was something strange that had come from the bottom of the tree, and it was lying next to the dead coyote. The wolf spirit walked next to Alex as he approached the strange item that was on the ground. Alex grabbed the item and discovered that it was a light-colored burlap bag. He opened it and found old shell casings, an old knife, bird feathers, a handwritten letter and an animal skull.

The skull had a huge bullet hole on the top of it, which piqued his interest. After looking closer at the animal skull, he realized that it belonged to a wolf. The random flashes of what the spirit wolf showed him in visions triggered a memory. This skull was supposed to be in the mound at the other end of the main path. The wolf's burial site had obviously been desecrated, which led to the spirit being trapped in limbo, unable to find peace. Alex held up his flashlight and opened the letter from within the burlap sack. The letter, dated 1895, said the following:

> *If this is found, put all of this back in the tree opening. The skull is from the small mound down the path. I talked to a local Indian who believed that the wolf in the mound aided the tribe that once lived here. They released some dark magic and that wolf haunted anyone trying to set up camp, or dig for land and the treasures of the Indian sites. We had enough of that demon*

and I found its skull with the help of the Indian and shot it twice. Taking it from the mound weakened it and trapped it here and it can't get us anymore. Put this back and cover it back up. You've been warned!

"Oh my God! This is awful!" Alex said aloud. He started walking to the end of the trail with the skull in his hands. The spirit wolf walked ahead of him, with its ghostly glow leading the way. Alex used his flashlight to scan the area and located the mound. The wolf spirit walked over to the spot where the rest of its body lay resting. Alex stood with the skull in his hands and watched the wolf lay down on its side, showing him where his skull was supposed to be placed. Alex found a sharp rock and began to dig into the mound and placed the skull back in its original place. After Alex covered it back up with dirt, the spirit wolf let out a long and haunting howl before vanishing into a white light and disappearing from the mound. As the spectral presence faded away, a profound stillness settled over the woods. Chillicothe, once haunted by the ghostly guardian, now felt a renewed sense of tranquility. The town's residents who were made aware were grateful for the brave efforts of Alex. They still share stories of the ghost wolf as a bittersweet memory of a guardian that had found peace at last.

WESTMORELAND PLACE

Westmoreland Place, formerly the original hospital in Chillicothe, Ohio, has a history rich with rumored ghostly encounters. Tales of eerie apparitions wandering the halls, strange sounds and inexplicable sensations have circulated among locals and visitors. Some claim to have seen spectral figures, heard ghostly whispers or felt an unexplained chill in certain areas of the building, especially the morgue. While these stories often lack concrete evidence, they contribute to the mystique and haunting reputation of the old hospital. Erected on the former grounds of the old Western Cemetery, the former Chillicothe City Hospital, which now operates as a rehabilitation center, may be haunted by those who were excavated from the graveyard that was once located there. This same cemetery was also the site of the legendary "clicking tombstone." Children who attended a nearby school refused to go near the grave marker due to the sound it made.

Melinda worked for the Westmoreland Place nursing facility and shared a chilling encounter with me about her time there. She had formed lifelong friendships with her coworkers and many of the residents. She treated them like family, and she was loved and cherished by those same residents. "It's finally Friday, girls!" she said to her coworkers in the nursing station. Melinda was finishing up her charts for the end of the week and was eager to log out of her computer. "Is it just me, or has Patti been acting a little off today? I hope she's not getting sick," one of the nurses said. Melinda had noticed something strange going on with Patti. She had been holding on to the walls, doorways and nurses station counter throughout the day in an attempt to support herself. Melinda thought that perhaps her medication was off, so as a precaution she began checking the charts and Patti's intake for the day. Melinda got up from her office chair to look for the medicine list so she could see what Patti was currently taking.

As she was turning each page to find any changes that had been made, Patti collapsed in the lobby near the activity room. Two of the nurses hurried over to Patti's side in an attempt to help her. She was unresponsive, not breathing and didn't have a pulse. The level of noise from the residents witnessing this ordeal and the nurses and doctor attempting to revive Patti caught Melinda's attention. She exited the records room and quickly walked toward the lobby and saw Patti on the floor, surrounded by nurses and a doctor. They were administering CPR and checking her vitals. Patti was still unresponsive. Melinda stood by the others and watched as they attempted to save her.

"Go on Patti! Get out of here! You're not allowed in here!" Melinda's attention was drawn away from what was happening in the lobby to a disturbance down the hall. She made her way down the hall to the room where the shouting was coming from. "I told ya Patti! Go on! Get out!" The sound of broken glass followed the demands from the resident in the room.

Melinda looked in and realized that it was Margaret's room. Patti and Margaret were always fighting and couldn't stand each other. "Get outta here Patti! Go on! Get out!" Margaret ordered Patti to leave her room, but Patti was still lying on the floor at the other end of the hall. Melinda stepped into the room to talk to Margaret and try to calm her down. *She must be having a nightmare during a nap*, she said to herself as she stepped inside. Melinda noticed that Margaret was sitting up in bed, wide awake and yelling in her direction. Margaret then said, "You need to get her out of the room! Patti isn't welcome!" She always accused Patti of stealing items from her room and looking through her drawers. Melinda realized that she'd better intervene and try to calm Margaret down. As she moved closer to the bed in an attempt to offer help, an overwhelming feeling of cold air filled the room. Melinda stopped moving, as the hair on the back of her neck stood on end. She looked in the direction where Margaret was yelling and throwing her shoes and remote. Melinda almost needed a seat after catching a glimpse of why Margaret was screaming.

Standing against the wall of the room was Patti. She just stood there, staring at Margaret as she screamed at her and threw things. Melinda couldn't believe what she was witnessing. Patti was in the room with her, and yet as she stepped back into the hallway, Patti was still on the floor there too. When Melinda stepped back into the room, Patti was standing near Margaret's bed and extending her hand, reaching for Margaret. She was becoming extremely agitated and screaming, "Go away Patti! You get out of here!" Patti started to slowly fade away into a mist, and then she completely disappeared. Within an instant, all was calm in Margaret's room. Melinda walked back out into the hall and noticed that a sheet had been placed atop Patti's lifeless body as the other nurses stood by crying.

Patti was gone. They couldn't revive her, yet somehow she was in two places at once. Melinda started walking back to the nurses' station and locked eyes with a few of the other nurses. She had a terrible poker face, so the other nurses could tell that something wasn't quite right. One of them approached Melinda and hugged her. "She went so quickly. I hope it was painless," the nurse said to her. Melinda started to think about what she had just experienced in Margaret's room. She wanted desperately to share her encounter with her fellow nurses, but she couldn't find the words. Melinda walked to her office chair and started to look for her belongings. She watched as the EMTs started to roll Patti out of the lobby and down the main hall.

Melinda started to feel sick and just wanted to go home and forget about the day's events. She couldn't stop thinking about what she had seen. Melinda started to wonder if perhaps she was losing her mind. She called in sick on Monday morning. Melinda did not want to go back to Westmoreland Place. The entire ordeal made her nervous and scared of every sound, shadow and howl of the wind. She returned to work a few days later and tried to go back to business as usual. Melinda eventually shared her encounter with a few of her closest coworkers. This opened a dialogue between her and other employees who had also experienced strange and paranormal happenings at Westmoreland Place. She eventually felt at peace with her experience and felt she could breathe freely once again. The few years that Melinda remained working for Westmoreland, she would often check in on Margaret, and they would share stories about Patti and how crazy her antics were. Melinda eventually moved on to another job, but she's kept the memories of her time there close to her heart.

ONE NIGHT IN THE MORGUE

In the dimly lit basement of Westmoreland Place, a once grand hospital now abandoned, a nurse named Sarah found herself on the unsettling periphery of the supernatural. Assigned to the night shift, her duties led her to the morgue, a cold and sterile chamber where the echoes of the past reverberated. One fateful night, Sarah received an urgent call to attend to the morgue. As she descended the creaking stairs, the temperature seemed to drop and an eerie silence enveloped the dimly lit corridor. The flickering lights cast unsettling shadows as she approached the heavy door marked "Morgue."

With a hesitant hand, Sarah pushed the door open, revealing rows of stainless steel tables that bore the weight of the departed. As she carried out her duties, a peculiar chill settled in the air and an inexplicable unease tingled down her spine. As Sarah meticulously worked, the soft sound of footsteps reached her ears. Startled, she glanced around, only to find the morgue empty. Brushing it off as her imagination, she continued with her tasks. However, the ghostly footsteps persisted, growing louder and more distinct. Suddenly, a child's laughter echoed through the sterile chamber, its innocence starkly out of place in the solemnity of the morgue. Sarah's heart raced as she spun around, searching for the source of the sound. To her astonishment, a ghostly figure materialized—a young child, pale and ethereal, standing at the edge of the room.

Wide eyed, Sarah locked eyes with the spectral child, whose presence seemed to defy the boundaries between the living and the dead. The ghostly child, adorned in an antiquated hospital gown, extended a translucent hand toward Sarah, a silent plea etched on its phantom face. In a hushed whisper, the ghost child shared a tale of longing and tragedy—a life cut short within the confines of Westmoreland Place. Sarah, overcome with a mix of empathy and terror, felt compelled to console the spirit, offering a semblance of comfort to the lingering soul. As Sarah reached out, the ghost child's form flickered, and the basement seemed to resonate with the echoes of a distant era. The child's laughter faded into the cold silence of the morgue, leaving Sarah alone in the dimly lit chamber.

Haunted by the encounter, Sarah continued her duties in the abandoned hospital, forever marked by the spectral visitation in the depths of Westmoreland Place. The morgue, a repository of both the living and the departed, stood as a chilling reminder of the unseen forces that lingered in the shadows of the past.

THE GHOST OF TIMMONS BRIDGE

In the mid-nineteenth century, a man by the name of Enos Kay lived along Egypt Pike in Ross County. This is an area on the outskirts of Ohio's first capital, Chillicothe. Enos was said to be a loyal and honest young man with a strong work ethic. Mr. Kay had become the envy of the entire region after having gained the attention of Alvira, a local and much desired young woman with a sharp mind, kind eyes and strong spirit. It took a few years for Enos Kay to save enough money for a wedding worthy of his beloved Alvira. It was almost as if she were patiently waiting for Enos to build his small fortune. When at last he saved up the money, wedding arrangements were soon underway. The wedding garments were designed and fitted, and everything was going well for the young couple until a fateful day in the spring of 1869 when they decided to attend a local church picnic. This was a community event where Enos could build rapport with other likeminded businessmen and perhaps expand his earning opportunities.

The story, according to many people from the area, stated that a mysterious and visually stunning stranger arrived at the picnic unannounced and uninvited. This man was not familiar to any of the churchgoers and just showed up at the church picnic that day. It was unclear what the man called himself—some of the picnickers thought his name was Mr. Smith, others thought it was Mr. Johnston and some even thought his last name was Brown. Many of the women blushed and smiled as they met his gaze, while the men were intimidated by his strong aura. The only thing they could all agree on was that the man clearly had eyes for the beautiful Alvira. Throughout the

Crossing the bridge. *Jaci Starkey.*

entire day, the stranger did his best to impress her and keep her attention while the meek and hapless Enos simply stood by and watched. Enos was not the jealous type, nor was he one who liked to engage in confrontation.

It didn't take long before rumors started to circulate that Alvira had been seen walking hand in hand with the handsome stranger. These rumors were dismissed by Enos as idle chatter and gossip. *How could Alvira, the love of my life, the woman who had promised her love to me, be with another man? That would be impossible!* he said to himself. The two of them had been courting for so long. To everyone's surprise, including his own, after returning a few days later from a business trip to the city, he was informed by a few friends and locals that the man was seen climbing through Alvira's bedroom window at night and that he had proposed to her. It was said that she had accepted and that they ran away together and got married. Enos was stunned and heartbroken.

He wasted no time running to his fiancée's house, where he discovered that Alvira had indeed left, gone forever. Enos let out a bloodcurdling cry from his heart; he swore that upon his death, he would forever haunt any happy lovers of this region until the end of time. After days of drinking and isolating himself, Enos Kay walked out to Timmons Bridge, which was where he proposed to Alvira. The locals had coined this covered bridge "the local lovers' lane." He hanged himself from the rafters of the bridge. Not long after Enos was mourned and buried, stories started surfacing of young lovers being terrorized at the bridge by some insidious, unseen force. Couples reported an evil and invisible force attacking their buggies by shaking them violently and scaring the horses. Some couples said that the malevolent force ripped open the tops of the buggies, revealing the demonic face of Enos Kay, peering down at them with death in his eyes.

Encounters with the ghost of Enos Kay are reported to this day. Apparently, he will not bother lone travelers passing over the bridge or a parked couple who are arguing instead of kissing. True to his oath, the tortured spirit claws and scratches at the parked cars of those couples who are expressing their love to each other. Some of these couples recall seeing the ghost's devilish grin through the steamed-up car windows. Enos Kay's kind heart and mild-mannered temperament have been replaced by despair, hate and rage.

THE EMPTY CABIN

I t was a period in time where those who needed a place to call their own could do so in whichever rusted-out abandoned shack they happened upon. It was the time of squatters. The year was 1964, and most of the residents within the outlying area of Chillicothe were suffering from the collapse of the coal mining industry and an ever-struggling economy. Mark was one of those not-so-fortunate children in a time when the system was not so fair and balanced. He was surrounded by poverty but raised with love. He was the youngest of four brothers, and like all good big brothers do, they made sure that Mark was tortured on a daily basis. Like so many times before, they were soon moving again. His father found a new job at a local sawmill, where his father's eldest brother worked alongside him in order to provide for their family. On a perfect late spring afternoon, while returning from work by way of an impromptu detour thanks to construction on the covered bridge, their father discovered their new home.

Their new dwelling came to a complete surprise to his mother, who had not yet finished boxing up their possessions. She grinned from ear to ear when her husband informed her that it was a log cabin that had been left untouched for years, with furniture and tools still inside. For them, moving was never that big of a deal. They lived a meager lifestyle, which made this type of an adjustment easy to handle. As a family, they were stitched well together. Within a few days, they hung their hats in a home that was new to them. Mark didn't expect a lot out of this new place and what it would provide for him. He had always been a straightforward kind of person who did as his parents instructed him and made the best out of what God gave him. This was his new home—a roof over his head, solid floors and electricity.

Like any child his age, he was eager to explore his new stomping grounds. A young boy's imagination has a tendency to run wild, but here was a moment when such wildness would be proven true. As the day turned into night in their new house, it seemed to grow colder, with the darkness looming from the natural canopy provided by the huge trees that surrounded the house. Mark was normally a heavy sleeper, but tonight was different. He had trouble sleeping thanks in part to his elder brothers making howling noises and knocking on the walls that separated his room from the others. He was not quite settled by the time he noticed it was midnight. The howling finally stopped, as did the knocking from his brothers—their mother made sure of that. He finally felt relaxed and ready to fall fast asleep.

Before he even had the chance, a new sound arrived. This time, it was coming from outside the house. He almost jumped out of his skin when he heard the faint sounds of footsteps on their front porch. He could hear the sounds of old, creaking wood as a result of heavy footsteps—*crack*, *pop*, *crack*, *creak*, *pop*. Then the house shook with a loud slam. This, of course, caught the attention of his father, who frantically ran down the stairs, with a shotgun in hand, prepared to unload on whoever was intruding in their home. As his father reached for the handle of the front door, he was startled by the fact that the door was still locked from the inside. He was troubled even further when he did not discover anyone outside or anywhere near their home.

The only ones who were completely aware of this fact were Mark, his father and Mark's elder brother Patrick. In order to prevent his mother from having a panic attack, they agreed to keep it from her. His father's eldest brother told his mother that it was just him opening windows to cool down the house. Six full days and six full nights went by quietly after that night. They managed to unpack and set up their belongings, as minimal as they were, throughout their house. As another bright and beautiful day turned to night, it had a strangely familiar feeling. Mark had not been that restless since that night a week before. This night felt slightly different from the one a week before though. The darkness was thick, the air was dry and the silence was deafening. Mark could hear his own heart pound as it pushed its way into his throat. It was becoming difficult to swallow as he began to search for new air to breathe. In a matter of minutes, just like clockwork, that same sound began to play itself again.

The same walk, the same creaking and popping, followed by an abrupt slam. This time was very different—not only did it prevent Mark from sleeping, but it also managed to wake everyone within the home. His mother was not as easily fooled this time. She had heard enough lies from her family and wanted the truth. "What was that? Who was that? I know it's not Robert! He's at Roy's tonight—they're fishing, Floyd! Who keeps doing this?" she cried out. Mark attempted to weave another lie, but his father felt that it was time to own up to the fact that he had no idea who or what kept doing it. He explained the situation to her and again checked the house. The story was the same—no one near the home and the door was locked. The remaining days within the week had the entire family on high alert. Mark had dreams of the fascinating things that could be causing the noises. However, when he relayed his ideas to his dad, they were quickly stifled. He was a skeptical man with grounded views. He was certain that it was either a wanderer, a couple of kids playing a joke or the original owner of the property trying to scare them away.

As the weekend approached, they felt as if they could breathe a little easier now that the last six days were behind them. In light of the bizarre events, Mark enjoyed his surroundings. His new home and the huge yard outside enabled him to play Lone Ranger and Tonto and even Batman and Robin with his brothers. The oak trees also provided nice cool spots to catch some sleep. For the third Sunday evening in the house, Mark, his eldest brother and their father concocted a plan for their unknown prowler. It was half an hour before midnight. Mark, his brothers and their parents piled into their car. The windows were down, and Mark was firmly planted between his parents in the front seat. They were ready to blow the horn as soon as they heard or saw something. His father was ready to pull the switch for the headlights as soon as something emerged from the shadows and set foot on their front porch.

They were going to give this intruder the scare of their life. They were going to frighten whomever it was more than the intruder had frightened them. As the second hand clicked toward midnight, the anticipation for what they were about to encounter was almost too much to withstand. The clock struck midnight, and at first it was dead silent. From behind them, they heard footsteps coming up the driveway—the sound of clunky boots on gravel was unnerving. They couldn't make out anything within the darkness. No one emerged, yet the sounds of footsteps became louder and closer. Then it turned into running. The sound ran past their vehicle, yet they could see no one. The sounds of footsteps were just like those two frightening nights.

The footsteps hit the planks of their front porch and, just like a skipping record, proceeded to re-create the same eerie sounds as the two times before.

They turned on their headlights in the hopes of catching a glimpse of someone, anyone who might be doing this to them. There was nothing before them, only the same haunting sounds that continued to play over and over again. As they heard the sound of a door slamming, they were shocked to realize that the front door remained closed despite the sound. The footsteps continued this time away from the house and back toward their vehicle and then stopped next to them. The phantom steps started up again. This time they moved into the woods. A ghostly melodic whistle, coming from lips that were not visible, accompanied the steps. Mark's father turned toward his family, a look of terror across his face. He clutched his gun tightly, double-checked to make sure all the doors in the car were locked and held fast to his family.

As soon as the sun peeked over the horizon of the hilltops, they all rushed inside. They gathered what they could run away with in their arms and piled into the car. Without so much as a quick glance goodbye, they turned their backs on this ghostly property that they had known as home for only a short while. The invisible intruder claimed its property once more without further protest from Mark and his family. The entire encounter left them shaken for longer than expected. It would take Mark months before the sounds of footsteps or a melodic whistling did not send him into a state of panic. From that moment on, Mark and his family made it a point to steer clear of abandoned shanties that were still fully furnished and appeared as if the original occupants fled from the property.

THE CURSE OF ELIZABETH'S GRAVE

The tragic tale of Elizabeth, an alleged witch, has been the cornerstone of ghost stories and paranormal yarns in the Chillicothe area since the 1800s. It is said that she is buried to the right of an oak tree from which she was hanged. Like many local legends, there are no written records pertaining to her having been alive or dead. Elizabeth and her mother were said to have fled from Salem, Massachusetts, in 1692 for the crimes of witchcraft. Elizabeth was supposed to have been fourteen or twenty at the time of her death in 1712. Elizabeth was only an infant when her mother fled with her from Salem.

They were said to be seeking refuge as far from the madness as possible. The two of them took a path in the area that went through the Erie Canal before it was commercialized during the industrial age. Elizabeth and her mother found a vacant house in the woods no more than one hundred feet from where the cemetery now rests. Elizabeth's mother was said to have befriended a local farmer. The farmer's first wife died in childbirth. The farmer took Elizabeth's mother as his wife after a long courtship. Elizabeth's mother never told her new husband about her supernatural abilities or where she came from; however, as Elizabeth grew into a young woman, it became evident to everyone in the area that both Elizabeth and her mother possessed special abilities.

This discovery led to their deaths at the hands of paranoid, angry people. With torches and pitchforks, the locals headed to the house that Elizabeth's mother had made into a home for them. The dying curse of a woman executed as a witch still haunts the grounds where these evil men accused her and sentenced her to death. Despite years of spirit communication by mediums and scientific tests with sophisticated equipment, no one has been able to eliminate the telltale imprint of the witch's mark from this region.

John Hicks was an important and politically powerful citizen in the Chillicothe area—so prominent, in fact, that Pleasant Valley, the village he founded, was named by him. The exact details of the events surrounding the murder of Elizabeth are hazy and have been lost due to the passage of time since her tragic death during the late seventeenth-century witchcraft hysteria in the New World.

The men and women murdered by their neighbors from Salem, as well as in states along the Southeast, are the most commonly remembered victims of the lethal religious hysteria that swept through the colonies during the early years of European settlement in America. Many others also died at the stake, were hanged by the noose or were crushed by boulders piled on their bodies in demented efforts to cleanse their souls of Satan and his demons. Elizabeth was one of the innocent victims whose slaying would have been forgotten if not for the agonized curse she pronounced on her tormentors moments before her death.

According to some accounts, Elizabeth's mother was a beautiful and alluring woman who had the misfortune of becoming the mistress of the arrogant and hardhearted John Hicks. When locals started talking about Elizabeth and her mother being witches, he got tired of her and wanted to end things. It's said that he arranged to have her accused by the church of witchcraft. Defenseless against the enmity of her former lover, she and her daughter were quickly convicted and condemned to death. Other tales claim that the victim of the black-hearted frontier bigwig was an unattractive crone who was typical of the victims selected for persecution during the witchcraft hysteria. She was old, eccentric, lived alone and was without friends or relatives to defend her. Still, other legends paint the victim as an Indian woman whose husband had been shot in the back by Hicks during a quarrel. According to some depictions from that era, Elizabeth was burned at the stake, and her mother's former lover personally ignited the wood piled at her feet after gutting her mother.

According to most accounts handed down through the centuries, Elizabeth was hanged from the oak tree and then buried beneath it. All the stories seem to agree, as well, that the last agonized words of the woman executed for witchcraft pronounced a terrible curse on Hicks and the locals who supported him. "Though you may slay me now, you dog," she croaked,

"I shall come back and dance upon all of your gravestones while you roast in hell." It was a powerful curse, uttered at a moment of extreme emotion and distress, and John Hicks didn't take it lightly. It haunted him throughout the remainder of his life, and members of his family shared his concern.

When he died, they took special care to select a perfect stone that was unblemished in any way for his final memorial. They called in the most respected stonemason in the area to shape the stone and carve the name of the family patriarch. As expected, John Hicks's tombstone was the finest of all those in the little cemetery. It seemed only proper, after all. On the anniversary of the accused witch's death, a curious thing occurred. The image of a woman dancing on Hicks's grave was witnessed by many locals. A tinged handprint with the color of rust, then with bright-red blood, began to form on the front surface of the once-perfect stone.

The good citizens of Ross County were horrified, but none so much as the family survivors of John Hicks. They ordered the stone sanded and cleaned again and again, but the image remained. The stone was sanded and cleaned more than a dozen times, but the image always returned within a few hours after the work was completed. At last, Hicks's heirs gave up on the stone and ordered a new one erected in its place. A few days after the new tombstone was placed on his grave, the image of the Elizabeth's handprint began to slowly form once more.

The second stone was removed and replaced with another clean rock slab, professionally formed by the best available stonemason and inscribed with John Hicks's name. Within a few days, the mystifying handprint again formed on the new stone. This time, the face of Elizabeth's mother appeared on the stone as well. The family members had to concede that they had enough, and they gave up. The third and final tombstone erected for John Hicks still stands in the cemetery outside Chillicothe, with the enigmatic form of the handprint deeply etched into the front surface, directly under his name.

Tortured Soul

Under the silver glow of a full moon, four friends set out on a curious adventure to Elizabeth's grave. The ancient cemetery exuded an eerie stillness as they approached the weathered tombstone, its inscription barely visible in the moonlight. As the friends gathered around, a sudden chill hung in the air and a faint mist materialized. A shadowy figure emerged, cloaked in a translucent sadness. The friends, initially startled, soon sensed a gentle longing emanating from the spirit that hovered before them. The melancholic apparition reached out, attempting to convey a tale obscured by time and tragedy. Whispers of a wrongful accusation, of Elizabeth being labeled a witch and meeting a tragic fate, echoed through the night. The friends, drawn into the spectral narrative, felt the weight of injustice that had befallen the spirit.

In an attempt to communicate, the ghostly figure manifested visions—scenes of a tight-knit community gripped by fear and suspicion, pointing accusing fingers at Elizabeth. The friends witnessed the tragic events that led to her unjust demise. Tears welled in the spirit's eyes, pleading for understanding and acknowledgment. As the friends listened, they became determined to uncover the truth surrounding Elizabeth's fate. Armed with empathy and curiosity, they decided to dive into the local historical records and archives the following day. They gradually pieced together the puzzle of her life and the unfounded accusations that had haunted her memory.

In their quest for justice, the friends discovered evidence in the form of letters and drawings that painted a different picture of Elizabeth—a compassionate spiritual healer misunderstood by a society clouded with fear and superstition. The community's misguided beliefs had led to her wrongful persecution and untimely death. With newfound knowledge, the friends returned to Elizabeth's grave, offering solace and a promise to share her true story. The once-saddened spirit, now bathed in a gentle light, expressed gratitude as it faded into the night, its lingering presence replaced by a sense of closure and peace. United by a spectral encounter and a shared commitment to righting the wrongs of the past, the friends left the cemetery with a profound understanding that sometimes the voices of the departed beckon to be heard, urging the living to unveil the truth that binds the living and the dead.

SHADOWS OF THE NIGHT

Under the cloak of night near Chillicothe, Ohio, a group of intrepid paranormal investigators gathered around Elizabeth's grave, drawn by whispers of spectral activity. Armed with ghost hunting equipment, they braved the moonlit cemetery, unaware that their search for the supernatural would awaken a malevolent force that had long slumbered in the shadows.

As the investigators initiated their paranormal inquiry, the air thickened with an unspoken anticipation. Eerie orbs danced in the moonlight, and the atmosphere crackled with an unnatural energy. Unbeknownst to the team, a collective of dark shadows, ancient entities resentful of intrusion, stirred beneath the gravestones.

Suddenly, the shadows coalesced into sinister forms, surrounding the investigators with an overwhelming darkness. Whispers, more chilling than the night wind, echoed through the graveyard as the shadows manifested their displeasure. The investigators, feeling an icy grip on their courage, realized that they were not alone in this spectral quest. The dark shadows, remnants of a forgotten era, surged forward, lashing out with ethereal tendrils. The investigators, now caught in a sinister dance between the living and the otherworldly, scrambled to fend off the encroaching darkness. Cries and moaning snaked through the air, enveloping the team in an ominous shroud. In the midst of the supernatural onslaught, the investigators clung to their purpose, determined to unravel the mysteries surrounding Elizabeth's grave. As they started to pray for peace and protection, they wielded their equipment as makeshift shields; the shadows intensified their assault, feeding off the fear that permeated the night.

Desperation fueled the investigators, and a surge of collective energy rippled through their ranks. With a burst of determination, they managed to pierce the veil between realms, momentarily dispersing the dark shadows. The graveyard fell silent, and the investigators, panting with exhaustion, surveyed the moonlit landscape. As the investigators retreated, the shadows, momentarily vanquished but not defeated, slinked back into the ancient recesses of the cemetery. Elizabeth's resting place, once again cloaked in quietude, became a testament to the unseen battles waged between the living and the shadows that guarded the realm of the departed.

The paranormal investigators, forever changed by the encounter, left the graveyard with a chilling tale of spectral resistance and a newfound awareness of the shadows that linger at the threshold of the supernatural. Chillicothe's haunted grounds stood as a reminder that some mysteries were best left undisturbed in the realm between the living and the shadows.

THE MADAM OF
LLOYD'S SWEET SHOPPE

L ong before Lloyd's Sweet Shoppe was a staple in the historical downtown district of Chillicothe, it stood as a charming relic with a dark past, having once been a clandestine brothel in the heart of the town. The ghostly legend that has surrounded that property is the tale of Madam Genevieve, a woman with a turbulent history whose spirit lingered, fueled by anger and unfulfilled desires. The unsuspecting candy store owners experienced peculiar incidents that hinted at the supernatural. The aroma of long-extinguished candles wafted through the air, faint echoes of laughter danced in the silence and occasional glimpses of a shadowy figure adorned in elegant Victorian attire unnerved the employees.

One fateful night, the owner, compelled by an otherworldly force, discovered a hidden compartment in the shop's basement. There were boxes of dusty old photographs and remnants of the brothel's past that unveiled Genevieve's tragic tale—a woman wronged by men who used her and her ladies of the night. Her life was cut short by betrayal and ruthless men who visited one night by way of the Erie Canal. Haunted by this revelation, the owner intended to unravel the mystery and help Madam Genevieve find peace. He adorned the shop with vintage décor reminiscent of its earlier days, creating an ambiance that seemed to calm the vengeful spirit. A secret alcove dedicated to Genevieve emerged, filled with candies and her personal belongings that she might have favored in life.

As the owner embraced the spectral presence, Genevieve's anger slowly transformed into a yearning for closure. Together, they revisited her past, uncovering the truths that had bound her spirit to the sweet shoppe. He would leave things out for her that he hoped would remind her of better times. With loyalty betrayed and love lost, Genevieve's anguish resonated through the corridors. In a poignant moment, the owner promised to honor her memory and acknowledge the pain she endured. As the promise echoed, the spectral Madam Genevieve began to dissipate, leaving behind a bittersweet energy that lingered like the faint scent of roses.

Lloyd's Sweet Shoppe was a harmonious blend of its sweet present and haunting past and became a place where locals sensed the ethereal presence of Madam Genevieve. The once angry ghost found solace, and the candy store transformed into a haven where history, both sweet and sorrowful, coexisted in a delicate balance. The owner continued running his store, occasionally catching glimpses of Genevieve's spirit, now more of a guardian than a ghost. The tale of Lloyd's Sweet Shoppe evolved into a town legend, a haunting with a resolution that bridged the gap between the living and the afterlife.

The Chillicothe Ghost Walk

The ghost walk of Chillicothe, Ohio, is an annual event that takes place every September. It's been a seasonal staple for this area since 2007. I've been actively involved with the ghost walk off and on for years as a storyteller, a guide, a paranormal expert and a public speaker. In 2008, I was working on setting up my display table with my books to sell, paranormal test equipment, ghostly merchandise, pamphlets and newspaper articles where I've been featured. I had already met with and spoken to the guides involved and other storytellers. Many of them were dressed in period clothing ranging from the Revolutionary era to Victorian times. I felt a little underdressed.

As I was setting everything up, a few people who were on the walk would stop by, talk to me and ask questions about the paranormal activity in this location. I was setting up on the floor directly above Lloyd's Sweet Shoppe. The upstairs area was being renovated at that time and being converted into apartments. Years before, it was used as a boarding school. It was also used as living quarters for people traveling with loads along the Erie Canal. That day, I was also informed that it once operated as a brothel. I was almost finished with hanging my banner and going over my notes when, out of the corner of my eye, I noticed a woman in a long black dress.

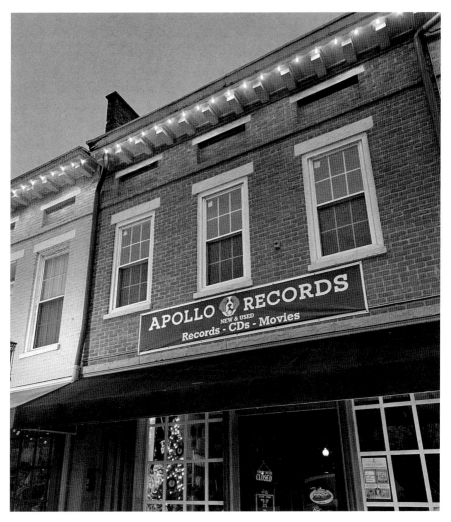

Ghost walk. *Neal Parks Photography*.

She was slowly gliding across the floor. The woman's hands were clasped together, and her head was down. This mystery woman wasn't making a sound as she moved past me. The dress that she wore appeared to be a thick, solid-stitched material. The neckline of her dress was made of a frilly, doily material, as were the ends of her sleeves. The woman wore a huge black hat with a large feather thoughtfully placed between a silk band at the section where the bill met the top. The feather dangled to the left of the back side of this hat. She was an older-looking woman; it's safe to say that she may have been in her late seventies.

While observing her, I was awestruck by how authentic her garb appeared to be. I wondered to myself whether or not she was the other guide assigned to the tour above Lloyd's. The thing that seemed the strangest during this encounter was the fact that as she walked past me, I did not hear footsteps—not even the shuffling of her feet. That strange, familiar feeling came over me, the feeling that I always get when I'm in the presence of something paranormal. I thought to myself that there's no way this woman was an apparition. I called out to her by introducing myself. "Hello, I'm Neal Parks, the paranormal researcher and author who will be working with you today." I extended my hand. There was no reply from her. I thought to myself, *Perhaps she had bad hearing.* I made another attempt at introducing myself, and this time I started walking toward her. The woman stopped at the doorway near the staircase; she appeared to be looking down at something. I called out to her again, "Hello," this time with a lot more inflection. "My name is Neal Parks. Are you the other tour guide?"

She did not respond. In fact, after I grabbed one of my electromagnetic meters and proceeded to approach her, she completely dissipated. I was in total disbelief. This woman appeared to be a solid being. She was no more than three feet from me during this encounter. I immediately walked through the doorway to see if perhaps she was around the corner or heading down the stairway. The woman was nowhere to be found. Throughout the rest of the ghost walk that day, I relayed that experience to every group and every person who came through to hear me speak. I certainly had one of the sweetest experiences above the candy shop that day.

A Haunting on Sugar Street

O n Sugar Street in Chillicothe, Ohio, among the quaint houses on the east end of town stands a foreboding structure that locals speak of in hushed tones. The old house, with its imposing presence, concealed a dark secret—an evil spirit that had long tormented its residents. Legend had it that the house harbored the vengeful ghost of a malevolent figure named Samuel Blackwood, whose wicked deeds in life had bound him to the mortal realm. As the sun dipped below the horizon, Sugar Street residents would close their curtains, fearful of the malevolent energy that emanated from the ominous mansion. Many people who take up residence in this property almost immediately move out. The home has become something of a curse, with numerous séances having been conducted, with Ouija boards being used by unsuspecting occupants.

The hauntings began innocuously with subtle noises—creaking floorboards, eerie whispers and inexplicable drafts. Soon, the malevolence escalated; shadows danced along the walls, and an icy chill pervaded the air even on the warmest days. Locals have avoided the house, yet the tales of the ghostly presence spread like wildfire.

Disembodied Voices

Trevor lived in the house on Sugar Street with his mother, stepdad and stepsister. "Oh great! You dragged us to Chillicothe and now a creepy house. It looks like a murder house," Trevor said as they started to unload their vehicle and take their items into the house. It was rumored that a man had killed his stepdaughter in the house and hid her body in the attic over the living room. Almost right away, they had several bizarre encounters in the house with doors and windows opening or closing, objects moving on the counters and many more strange things. His room and his stepsister's bedroom were on the second floor over the kitchen. There was a small hatch in her room leading to the attic above the living room. One night, his stepsister and her friends decided that they were going to go into the attic and look around. Trevor watched as she and her friends went through the hatch.

After close to five minutes, the door slammed shut. All of them started to scream and pound on the walls and the hatch door. Trevor rushed over to pull the door open, but it wouldn't budge. He started to panic, thinking that his parents would think that he locked them in there. Trevor started to kick hard at the door in an attempt to open it. He grabbed his sister's curling iron, jammed the flat end into the crevice in the corner of the doorframe and pried open the door. The girls came tumbling out from the opening, and two of the girls were so terrified and shaken by what they had seen that they begged for their parents to come and pick them up.

Trevor's stepsister, Molly, was as white as a sheet, and her hair was a mess. He asked them what happened, but she wouldn't tell him. She just sat there, staring at the opening and breathing fast and heavy. One of the other girls spoke up when Trevor's mom walked in and asked, "What in the world is going on in here? It sounds like you're going to come through the ceiling!" All of them looked at her as she entered the room.

The girl said, "It was awful! There was a man's body, but it had a dog head instead of a human head. It kept hunching over and crawling on all fours chasing us around!"

Trevor and Molly's mother looked at all of them. "This is your doing isn't it, Trevor? You just had to scare everyone!" she said.

Trevor spoke up, defending himself against this baseless accusation. He was livid. "I did not! I'm the one who got the door open. It slammed shut on its own!" He stood his ground and waited for a rebuttal.

One of the other girls spoke up. "He's telling the truth! I looked back before the door slammed. He was nowhere near it. He stood there against the wall when that happened." Trevor smiled at Molly's friend as she offered her eyewitness testimony.

Their mother had calmed down by this point and responded, "A man with a dog head? In there? That's what all of you saw?" The girls shook their heads collectively. A few of the girls went home, traumatized by what they had encountered, while half of them decided to go ahead and stay the night as planned.

As the night progressed, the girls were watching TV in the living room while Trevor sat in the next room reading a book. He couldn't sleep after what had just happened. His nerves were shot, and he didn't want to leave the girls alone downstairs. After things felt a little more calm and normal, they heard a window slam upstairs and their mother scream. They all ran upstairs and found their mother curled up in a ball on her bed. They asked her what happened, and she said that she had been reading when she looked over to the window and saw a woman in a white dress and no legs. She said that the woman said to her, "Mary, it's time to come home," and then the window slammed shut. At that moment, they decided that everyone was sleeping downstairs with the lights on and close together.

They Weren't My Parents

The first time I was home alone in this creepy house, I was playing video games in my room. While I was heavily involved in a game, I heard a man's voice at the bottom of the stairs in the dining room. I was startled by that, considering that my parents had left hours ago and were going to be gone for a few hours more. The voice said, "Did you remember to get the beer?" I then heard a woman's voice say, "No." I sat up straight and said to myself, "That sounds like mom and dad, but is it?" I peeked around the corner and slowly made my way to the edge of the stairs. I descended downstairs and realized that no one was in the house. The TV in the living room came on by itself, and I could hear heavy footsteps in the attic above. The steps went the entire length of the attic and then stopped. This was followed by the sound of a little girl crying. I started to feel what would be best described as an "evil presence." Without hesitation, I made my way to the front door and out of the house, heading to my friend's house for the rest of the evening.

PARANORMAL EXPLORERS

Emily was a courageous young woman fascinated by the supernatural. Intrigued by the stories surrounding the house on Sugar Street, she decided to unravel the mysteries within its walls. The house sat empty for months. It was a perfect time to investigate. Armed with test meters, a flashlight, camera equipment and a determination to confront the paranormal, Emily crossed the threshold with a few friends into the abyss.

As they explored room after room, she encountered the restless spirit of Samuel Blackwood. His malevolent presence filled the air, and his spectral form materialized, exuding an aura of pure evil. Unfazed, Emily delved into the tragic past that had forged Samuel's vengeful spirit—a tale of greed, hopelessness and a life cut short in the pursuit of dark desires. Rather than succumbing to fear, Emily and her friends called out to Samuel with empathy. She acknowledged the pain that had bound him to the earthly plane and pleaded for him to find peace. Samuel's rage wavered as he listened to Emily's heartfelt words, and for the first time, a glimmer of humanity flickered in his spectral eyes. "You remind me of the daughter I lost," the spirit whispered to her. Emily's compassion was not able to break the shackles that bound Samuel to the house. The dark energy had become a vessel of evil and vengeance.

Emily felt that it would be a good idea to try to cleanse this bitter spirit. She started to say a prayer as her friends joined hands with her. Samuel warned them that they were no longer welcome and that it was too late for him. "You have to go now!" Samuel said with rage. Their attempt to help this angry soul was in vain. Samuel had become the dark and evil phantom that everyone had feared. At that moment, items that were boxed and still sitting in the house were tossed from left to right, and pictures hanging from the walls were ripped away and thrown across the room. Emily and her friends wasted no time running from the house. They regrouped on the sidewalk and realized that they may have made it worse. The house on Sugar Street remains a haven for darkness and should be avoided.

THE HILLS ARE ALIVE

In the serene landscape of the Huntington Hills in Ross County, Ohio, a spectral unrest lingered. The rolling hills, once a silent witness to the tumultuous past, concealed a tale of betrayal that fueled the anger of Civil War ghosts. The vengeful spirits sought revenge for the desecration of their final resting places. As dusk settled over the hills, a spectral army emerged from the shadows. These angry apparitions were remnants of soldiers who had fought valiantly during the Civil War only to meet a dishonorable fate in death. Their graves, scattered and displaced, fueled a rage that transcended time. These were the graves of freed slaves who had not only fought for their freedom but also helped in freeing slaves from the Southern states still trapped in servitude. This was a cemetery used for Black Union soldiers; at that time in history, they were never permitted to be buried in "white" cemeteries.

Many of the homes in that area had been affected by these paranormal encounters. A few of the homes were haunted by the spirits of these soldiers. There were stories of phantom whispers in these houses and shadows that were seen moving along the walls from room to room. Over the years, families would move into these homes and then move out almost as quickly. The stories of this specific area started to spread like wildfire. People started looking into what was causing these disturbances, and it was revealed that years before, when the area was being cleared and excavated for home builders, a hidden cemetery was uncovered. The company clearing the area decided not to report the discovery and continued with the project.

"The Hills Are Alive." *Kristin Parks Photography*.

Rebecca was a Civil War historian with a passion for uncovering the untold stories of the past. Intrigued by the whispers of the vengeful spirits, she embarked on a quest to understand their grievances and, if possible, offer them the peace they had been denied. Guided by an ethereal energy, Rebecca traced the history of the fallen soldiers. She discovered that unscrupulous individuals had plundered their graves, scattering their remains to obscure the true extent of the sacrifice made during the Civil War. The ghosts, bound by the injustice, sought retribution.

Determined to right the wrongs of the past, Rebecca enlisted the help of a few locals who shared her reverence for history. The small group worked to locate and restore the scattered graves of the fallen soldiers. The spirits, initially skeptical, observed the efforts with spectral vigilance. With each rediscovered grave, the atmosphere in Huntington Hills shifted. The vengeful ghosts, once consumed by anger, began to manifest a somber calmness. Rebecca, in a poignant moment, addressed the spectral army, acknowledging the betrayal they had suffered and expressing gratitude for their sacrifices.

The ethereal realm resonated with the echoes of forgiveness as the angry Civil War ghosts, now appeased, dissolved into the misty hills. Huntington Hills, once haunted by the wrath of the forgotten soldiers, became a place of serenity and remembrance. Rebecca's efforts turned the tale of vengeance into a town legend, emphasizing the importance of honoring the sacrifices of the past. The hills, once haunted by the angry spirits seeking revenge, now stood as a testament to the resilience of history and the power of redemption.

SPIRITS OF THE WOODS

In the heart of Huntington Hills, where ancient trees whispered secrets and the air hummed with a mystical energy, a father and his young son embarked on a traditional hunting expedition. Little did they know that the spirits of the woods were watching over them, guardians of the natural realm ready to intervene when nature took a dark turn. As the father and son ventured deeper into the dense forest, the tranquil atmosphere shifted. Sinister howls echoed through the trees, signaling the presence of a pack of hungry coyotes closing in on the unsuspecting hunters. The duo, unaware of the imminent danger, continued their journey, the forest growing quieter as the predators prepared to strike.

Suddenly, the air shimmered with an otherworldly glow as ethereal figures emerged from the depths of the woods. The spirits of the woods, guardians of the delicate balance between nature and humanity, took form. Wisps of light and shadow danced around the father and son, creating an invisible barrier that shielded them from the impending threat. The coyotes, sensing

"Trail of Terror." *Kristin Parks Photography.*

the mystical intervention, hesitated at the edge of the protective aura. The spirits, ancient and wise, communicated with the creatures through a language transcending the earthly realm. A silent understanding passed between the spirits and the coyotes, and the pack retreated into the shadows, their hunger momentarily appeased.

The father and son, now aware of the supernatural intervention, stood in awe as the spirits of the woods bestowed on them a silent blessing. Nature's guardians, with eyes reflecting the wisdom of centuries, faded back into the ancient trees, leaving the hunters unharmed but profoundly changed by the encounter. As the father and son continued their journey, the woods seemed to embrace them with a renewed sense of harmony. The whispers of leaves and the murmur of the wind conveyed gratitude from the spirits that had intervened to protect those who entered their sacred domain.

From that day forward, the tale of the spirits of the woods in Huntington Hills spread through the community, a reminder of the mystical guardians that watched over the delicate dance between humanity and nature. The father and son, forever touched by the ethereal encounter, held a newfound respect for the unseen forces that weave through the heart of the ancient forest.

THE GUARDIAN OF MAIN STREET

A historic house in downtown Chillicothe was at one time the face of a coffin making company. Over the years, the property changed hands many times and, most recently, has been operating the last several years as a well-respected optometrist office. Years after the coffin making company closed and the house was sold and converted into three separate apartments, the house was known for strange and otherworldly happenings. People who were living in the apartments shared stories of hearing disembodied voices, seeing shadow beings move along the wall and encountering phantom odors. In the quiet solitude of Ms. Eleanor's apartment within this historic home, a mysterious presence lingered unseen by the living. Eleanor, an older woman with a heart full of stories and a spirit weathered by time, lived alone in her cherished abode. Little did she know that a chilling night would bring forth an unexpected guardian from the other side.

As the clock ticked away, she realized that it had gotten very late. Eleanor placed her book on the nightstand and shut off her lamp. It became calm and silent as she was trying to drift off to sleep. Eleanor was completely unaware that a shadowy figure had crept into her home, intent on robbing her. The intruder, masked by darkness, moved stealthily through the creaking halls, unaware that a spectral entity watched from the shadows. Eleanor was still awake at this point and felt that something wasn't right. She slowly sat up in bed and looked down the hallway. The moonlit night provided a small amount of light, enabling her to see. Suddenly, a ghostly figure materialized—the guardian angel of the house.

Carlisle Building. *Neal Parks Photography.*

This benevolent spirit, once a resident of the very home Eleanor now occupied, felt a duty to protect its former haven and its current inhabitant. Wisps of cold air filled the room as the ghostly presence confronted the intruder. A sudden gust extinguished the dim glow of the intruder's flashlight, leaving them disoriented and vulnerable. Distinct whispers echoed through the air, conveying a spectral warning to leave this sacred space. Startled, the intruder hesitated, sensing an unseen force working against their sinister intentions. With an otherworldly strength, the ghost created an eerie display of flickering lights and faint whispers, disorienting the intruder further. Meanwhile, Eleanor, sitting up at full attention in her bed, felt an inexplicable sense of reassurance as the paranormal intervention unfolded.

The intruder, overwhelmed by the ghostly encounter, hastily fled the scene, leaving the house in an anxious silence. As dawn approached, Eleanor discovered no signs of the trespasser, only a lingering feeling of gratitude for the unseen guardian that had intervened on her behalf. From that night forward, Eleanor shared her home with a silent protector—a benevolent ghost that had once lived within the walls and now safeguarded her in the twilight between the living and the afterlife. The bond between the spectral guardian and Ms. Eleanor served as a testament to the enduring connections that transcend the boundaries of mortality. As I mentioned earlier in this story, this property is now an optometrist's office. Many employees have shared stories with me of having encounters with a male spirit while on the second floor. They've said that they do not feel threatened by this apparition. They feel that he's like a protector.

THE EVIL WITHIN

In the picturesque town of Chillicothe, Ohio's first capital, a chilling tale has been shared through the years, casting a shadow over the quaint streets and historic buildings. It all began with the arrival of a young artist named Margaret, who moved into an old brick house on the outskirts of town. Little did she know that the past held a malevolent secret within its timeworn walls. Margaret had hired help with renovations in the kitchen, bathroom and guest room. As she immersed herself in her artwork, strange occurrences disrupted the serenity of her new home. Unexplained whispers echoed through the halls as she would try to sleep, and an unsettling coldness permeated the air. Unfazed, Margaret dismissed these phenomena as mere quirks of an old house or just her sleep-deprived imagination. She was not only working on a few larger pieces, but she was also trying to unpack boxes, update the home and settle in.

Late one ominous night, as she was preparing for an earlier than normal bedtime, an apparition materialized in the dim glow of Margaret's studio. It was a tormented figure. The ghost bore the anguish of a forgotten tragedy. It was the spirit of Marcus Dalton, a slave who had met a grisly end while hiding during the age of the Underground Railroad. He died within these very walls more than a century before. Consumed by a malevolent force, Marcus had become an entity driven by hatred and a thirst for vengeance. Marcus targeted Margaret, mistakenly blaming her for the sins of the living. The once charming house transformed into a haunting ground where shadows whispered accusations and the air grew heavy with a malignant presence.

Margaret often tried to have friends over for dinner or just to hang out. Her attempts were met with disruption and embarrassment. She became known as the girl with the ghosts. It was becoming harder for her to make friends thanks to the rumors and stories going around about her haunted house and the dark energy within it. Margaret, increasingly tormented by spectral nightmares and unsettling encounters, sought the help of a paranormal investigator. They met at the library and historical society with plans to dive deep into the town's archives, uncovering the tragic tale of Marcus Dalton's murder. These meetings went on for a few days and into the following weekend. It was revealed that he was betrayed and slain by someone he once trusted, leaving his soul restless and vengeful. The house was supposed to be a safe place, but it was turned into a pit of hell for Marcus.

As Margaret faced the wrath of Marcus's vengeful spirit, she desperately wanted to unravel the mystery and bring peace to the tormented soul. She noticed that he seemed to be more active and agitated during the evening hours, so Margaret decided to sit and wait. She made plans with the investigator and their research team to come over the next evening in an attempt to flush Marcus out. Plans changed due to a more hostile than usual confrontation. The truth was unveiled, exposing the betrayer who had condemned Marcus to an eternity of wrath. Marcus placed his hand on her forehead, and the events from the past started to play like an old home movie. Margaret's eyes started to fill with tears as she came to a full understanding of what happened to Marcus. With the revelation of the betrayal, Marcus's spirit, no longer tethered by hatred, found a solemn release. He felt understood and cared about. The shadows lifted, and the house, once shrouded in a spectral gloom, returned to its tranquil state. Margaret, forever marked by the ghostly encounter, continued her artwork and renovations with a newfound respect for the lingering echoes of the past in the town of Chillicothe.

It's Above the Men's Shop

Late one fog-laden night in Chillicothe, the local police received an unusual distress call from the owner of the property that housed the Men's Shop and Bob's Bootery. Reports from its surveillance described eerie noises, strange occurrences on the upper floors of the building and a small boy showing up on the security cameras, prompting a skeptical yet curious response from the officers. It didn't take too long for them to arrive since they were only two blocks away. As the officers ascended the creaking staircase, an unsettling chill enveloped the air and the distant echoes of footsteps reverberated through the silent halls. The flickering glow of their flashlights barely penetrated the thick veil of darkness that clung to the upper floors.

Both officers stood in place and just listened for a few minutes. One of the officers called the business owner to ask if he was seeing anything on the cameras that they weren't aware of. He was shocked when the owner told him that a little boy was standing right next to them. The police officer stepped back a few paces and shined his light along the wall, instructing the other officer to do the same. The owner was getting annoyed at this point and asked, "Are you blind, officer? He's right in front of you. How do you not see him?" The other officer started to get very nervous and said, "I'm done with this! Whatever is here doesn't want us to see it! It's not normal, Sarge!" Suddenly, a ghostly figure materialized before them—a translucent boy, his eyes filled with a mixture of innocence and sorrow. The officers, initially taken aback, soon realized that the apparition bore no ill will. Instead, he seemed lost, caught between realms.

Top floor. *Neal Parks Photography*.

The ghostly boy, clad in vintage clothing from a bygone era, pointed toward a stack of boxes in the corner. The officers slowly approached the stack and noticed dusty old photographs inside of the top box. One depicted a lively scene of children playing in front of the Men's Shop and Bob's Bootery many decades before. The officers, connecting the dots, realized that the spectral presence before them was a child from the past, lingering in search of something left unfinished. The younger officer realized that one of the children in the collection of pictures was that same small boy. Driven by a mix of fear and compassion, the police officers decided to investigate the building's history. Days later, through dusty archives and faded newspaper clippings, they uncovered a heartbreaking tale of the young boy who had met an untimely end while in the vicinity. He had died during the flu outbreak of 1918. His name was Isaac, and he died along with thirty other children. The officers had a newfound understanding. As they gently approached the ghostly boy many nights later, they offered reassurance and empathy. They spoke the child's name and told him that it was okay to let go and safe to move on. The child's features reflected a mix of relief and gratitude, and he dissipated into the unknown, leaving behind a lingering sense of closure.

The two police officers, now witnesses to the paranormal, shared a silent acknowledgment of the inexplicable events that had unfolded. The upper floors of the Men's Shop and Bob's Bootery, once haunted by a spectral presence, returned to a tranquil stillness. The small town, forever touched by this encounter, continued its quiet existence, with residual haunts from years before and whispers of the ghostly boy becoming a part of local lore.

THE SPIRIT OF THE GUESTHOUSE

Nestled in the heart of the charming town of Chillicothe, there stood an old inn known as the Guesthouse Bed and Breakfast. Guests flocked to this quaint establishment for its timeless charm and warm hospitality, but there was one unique aspect that set it apart: the presence of a friendly spirit named Garret. He was a benevolent and playful apparition and had made the inn his eternal home. He found joy in making the guests' stays memorable by adding a touch of the supernatural to their experiences. With a mischievous spirit, Garret had a penchant for snuggling up to guests in the night, wrapping them in a kind embrace that left them feeling comforted rather than frightened.

Many guests recounted waking up to the sensation of a gentle presence beside them, a phantom snuggle that brought an unexpected sense of warmth. Far from being scared, those who encountered Garret spoke of feeling a sense of peace and reassurance, as if the spirit was there to offer solace to weary travelers. Garett's playful antics extended beyond snuggling. He took pleasure in rearranging small items in the rooms. Guests would wake up to find their belongings subtly moved—a book placed on a different nightstand, a pair of shoes neatly aligned in a row and so on. Instead of causing alarm, Garret's actions sparked conversations among guests, fostering a sense of camaraderie as they shared their encounters with the friendly spirit.

The innkeepers, aware of Garret's presence, embraced him as part of the Guesthouse's charm. They would often hear delighted laughter echoing through the halls as Garret engaged in his spectral games with the guests. The spirit became a cherished and endearing aspect of the bed-and-breakfast, adding an extra layer of magic to the historic inn. Over the years, the legend of Garret, the friendly snuggling spirit, spread far and wide. The Guesthouse Bed and Breakfast became a destination not just for its charming rooms and delicious breakfasts but also for the chance to experience the warm and otherworldly presence of a playful ghost.

Guests continued to visit, hoping for a night of spooky snuggles and lighthearted surprises, carried out by the friendly spirit that had found eternal joy in making the living feel at home in his spectral embrace. The Guesthouse Bed and Breakfast, with its charming blend of the past and the paranormal, stood as a testament to the enchanting coexistence of the living and the dearly departed.

HOLIDAY PARTY

Amid the festive holiday party at the Guesthouse Bed and Breakfast in Chillicothe, laughter and warmth filled the air. As the night unfolded, a hushed murmur was spreading among the guests as they claimed to hear mysterious voices emanating from both the basement and the chimney. It sounded like people laughing and calling out the guests by name. A few of the guests wondered if perhaps their own echoes were causing the anomaly. It took a few minutes before everyone would calm down long enough and remain silent in order to hear the mysterious sounds. The voices were clearer and more pronounced. The voices from the chimney sounded like a cry for help, while the voices coming from the basement sounded like a group of people having a party and singing.

Curiosity lured a small group to look in and around the chimney, as another group investigated the basement, where they uncovered old relics and traces of a bygone era. Whispers lingered in the air, and tales of the guesthouse's history emerged. The voices coming from the chimney stopped after one of the guests called out to whomever was in the chimney. The following day, the echoes of the previous night were still fresh when a guest strolling through the garden and courtyard encountered a spectral figure in a soldier's uniform, seemingly from the early 1900s. Surprised, she called out to him, but as quickly as he appeared, he vanished into the shadows.

Rumors spread among the guests, linking the mysterious voices, the soldier and the rich history of the bed-and-breakfast. Some speculated that the soldier was a ghost from the past, perhaps a residual echo of the flu outbreak of 1918.

The atmosphere in Chillicothe's Guesthouse took on an enchanting quality, blending the holiday festivities with a sense of mystery. Guests couldn't help but wonder if the spirits of the past were joining the celebration, leaving them with an unforgettable holiday tale to share for years to come.

DEATH OF A MAID

Along the halls of the nineteenth-century Guesthouse, psychic Franny Starling embarked on a journey into the past. The air seemed to thicken as she closed her eyes, focusing on the spiritual energies surrounding her. Suddenly, a presence materialized—the tormented spirit of a maid who met a tragic end. As Franny connected with the mysterious entity, chilling sensations overwhelmed her. The ghostly apparition conveyed the tale of betrayal and murder that unfolded decades ago. The maid, named Abigail, had been romantically involved with the owner of the home, but their affair came at a steep cost. Franny, now immersed in Abigail's memories, felt the hands of the murderer around her own neck, the malicious intent palpable. The sensation of being pushed down a flight of stairs left her breathless, even in the safety of the present.

Abigail's spirit, desperate for justice, revealed the shocking truth: the murderer was none other than the wife of the home's owner. In a fit of jealousy and rage, she discovered the affair and decided to end it brutally, shattering the lives of all involved. Haunted by the revelations, Franny knew that she had a responsibility to bring closure to this spectral tragedy. With her psychic abilities, she sought out records, letters and stories that had been passed down through the generations validating the events Abigail had shared. The collection of evidence confirmed a maid's untimely demise in the 1840s, but the details of the murder were obscured by time.

With the assistance of a local historian and her fellow researchers, they pieced together the puzzle, uncovering the painful secrets that had long been buried. Armed with this newfound knowledge, she held a séance and a prayer session within the very halls where the tragedy occurred, inviting the spirits involved to find solace. As the séance unfolded, the atmosphere crackled with energy, and the ghostly figure of Abigail manifested once more. In an ominous glow, she confronted the wife's spirit, demanding justice. The air became heavy with tension as the guilty spirit confessed to the heinous crime, revealing the depths of her jealousy and resentment.

With this revelation, Abigail's spirit found a measure of peace, and the atmosphere within the guesthouse lightened. Franny, exhausted but fulfilled, felt a profound connection to the past and a sense of closure for the lingering spirits. The psychic left the historic guesthouse, leaving behind a place forever changed by the revelations of its dark past. Abigail's story, once lost in the shadows of time, now served as a testament to the enduring power of psychic intuition and the pursuit of justice, even from beyond the veil.

TOO COLD FOR GHOSTS

In the winter of 1978, Chillicothe, Ohio, found itself in the icy grip of a relentless blizzard. Snowflakes, like frozen whispers, descended on the town, blanketing streets and houses in a pristine white. As the snow piled higher, the community huddled indoors, leaving only the bravest souls to endure the storm. Among those courageous souls was Officer Harris, a seasoned police officer with a heart as sturdy as his cruiser. Assigned to patrol the desolate streets during the blizzard, he ventured into the frozen landscape, his headlights piercing through the swirling snowflakes.

The wind howled, and the streets were eerily silent, except for the muffled hum of the police cruiser. Officer Harris, bundled in layers against the biting cold, peered through the frosted windshield, his breath forming clouds in the frigid air. His mission: to clear the deserted streets, ensuring the safety of those who had chosen to weather the storm at home. As he drove through the desolate town, Officer Harris's vigilant eyes caught a peculiar sight ahead. A figure, tall and imposing, emerged from the swirling snow, casting a long shadow on the frozen ground. Intrigued and cautious, he slowed the cruiser, focusing on the silhouette that walked gracefully through the blizzard.

To his astonishment, the figure took form—an ethereal giant, a ghostly Indian with features outlined by the shimmering snow. The spirit, adorned in tribal attire, moved with a serene yet purposeful grace. Officer Harris, both captivated and bewildered, watched in awe as the ghostly figure crossed the path of his cruiser. In the midst of the blizzard, a silent communion occurred between the living and the spectral. The towering ghost, a guardian of the land, seemed to acknowledge Officer Harris with a nod, as if blessing his efforts to keep the town safe amid the tempest.

As quickly as it appeared, the ghostly figure vanished into the icy haze, leaving Officer Harris with a sense of wonder and reverence. With renewed determination, he continued his patrol through the blizzard, guided not only by the glow of his cruiser's headlights but also by the ethereal encounter that unfolded amid the snow-covered streets of Chillicothe, Ohio.

DEATH'S REFLECTION

In the heart of downtown, nestled within an old house, there stood a mirror with an ominous reputation. This seemingly ordinary looking glass held a dark secret—it possessed the power to reveal glimpses of one's inevitable demise. The giant home, with its creaking floorboards and faded wallpaper, had a storied history, but the haunted mirror, perched in an ornate frame, stood as the focal point of otherworldly mystery. Legend spoke of those who dared to gaze into its depths, only to witness haunting visions of their own demise.

One fateful evening, a curious young woman named Candy Mills inherited the mansion from a distant relative. Intrigued by the tales surrounding the mirror, she couldn't resist the temptation to unlock its secrets. As the moonlight bathed the room in an ethereal glow, Candy stood before the mirror, her reflection flickering in the antique glass. A shiver ran down her spine as the room seemed to grow colder. The mirror's surface rippled with an otherworldly energy, revealing a vivid image of Candy's future demise. The vision unfolded like a macabre tapestry—shadows, premonitions and echoes of the inevitable.

Undeterred by fear, Candy, with a mix of courage and curiosity, delved into the mystery of the mirror. Each reflection unveiled a different facet of her fate, creating a chilling mosaic that left her questioning the choices she would make. As whispers of the haunted mirror spread through the town, locals were drawn to the house, eager to glimpse their own destinies. Some recoiled in horror, unable to bear the weight of the revelations, while others faced their reflections with a solemn acceptance. Amid the growing intrigue, an older woman named Eliza visited the house. With a twinkle in her eye, she approached the mirror, recognizing it as a conduit between realms. Eliza, well versed in paranormal studies, whispered an ancient prayer in Latin, hoping to lift the veil of darkness that clung to the haunted glass.

As the prayer resonated through the room, the mirror's malevolent energy waned. Its surface ceased to reveal foreboding visions, and a sense of calm settled on the old house. The haunted mirror, now stripped of its ominous power, stood as a silent witness to the transformative journey it had guided people through. Candy, grateful for the wise intervention, decided to keep the mirror as a reminder of the delicate balance between destiny and choice. The mansion, once shrouded in mystery, now harbored a newfound sense of tranquility, with the haunted mirror transformed into a symbol of resilience and the ability to shape one's fate.

THE DINNER PARTY

During a calm winter in the 1930s, a grand dinner party was planned in one of the larger houses in Chillicothe, Ohio. As guests gathered in the opulent dining room, the air buzzed with laughter, clinking glasses and the clatter of fine china. Among the elegant attendees were friends, socialites and a curious relic—a mysterious, ornate mirror that had been passed down through generations. As the night progressed, the flickering candlelight cast a warm glow over the room. Many guests were asking about the gorgeous antique mirror and took turns looking into it, making faces and teasing each other over their reflections. The conversation flowed freely until someone noticed an unfamiliar reflection in the antique mirror. Gasps filled the room as one by one, guests saw the apparitions of their long-lost loved ones, who seemed to peer back at them through the glass from the realm beyond.

The atmosphere shifted, and a hushed reverence enveloped the gathering. Tears welled in the eyes of those who beheld the spectral images of parents, siblings and friends who had departed this world. The haunted mirror, a conduit between the living and the dead, unveiled a poignant reunion that transcended the boundaries of time. Yet as the night moved along, the joyous reunion took a haunting turn. Shadows lurking in the corners of the room grew menacing, and the once-welcoming apparitions twisted into dark, foreboding figures. Whispers of long-forgotten tragedies echoed through the air, sending shivers down the spines of the unsuspecting guests.

The grandeur of the evening crumbled as the spirits transformed into malevolent entities, chasing the partygoers from room to room. Panic set in as the once celebratory atmosphere devolved into a nightmarish ordeal. Desperate to escape the encroaching darkness, the guests fled the haunted mansion, leaving behind the chilling echoes of a supernatural encounter. The house, now shrouded in an eerie stillness, stood as a silent witness to the events that had unfolded.

The haunted mirror, having revealed both the beauty and horror of the afterlife, returned to its reflective slumber, awaiting the next curious soul who dared to peer into its haunted depths. The mirror was soon removed and placed in storage. The tale of the ill-fated dinner party became a whispered legend in Chillicothe, a cautionary reminder that sometimes, even the most cherished relics can harbor secrets that blur the line between the living and the dead.

RESTLESS SPIRITS OF THE ELKS LODGE

In the heart of Chillicothe, the Elks Lodge stands as an imposing structure, cloaked in history and secrets. Beneath its grand façade, a shadowy past lingered, intertwined with mediums who once sought to communicate with the dead, unknowingly releasing spirits that would haunt the property for years to come. More than a century before, a group of mediums gathered within the dimly lit chambers of the Elks Lodge, their séances attempting to bridge the gap between the living and the deceased. With candles flickering in the darkness, they channeled energies beyond their comprehension, releasing forces that should have remained undisturbed.

As the mediums delved deeper into their spiritual endeavors, the Elks Lodge became a focal point for supernatural activity. Ghostly apparitions roamed the halls, their ethereal moans echoing through the silent chambers. It was said that the mediums had unwittingly unleashed not only benevolent spirits but also malevolent entities that lurked in the shadows. Over the years, reports of eerie encounters proliferated among the lodge's members. Late-night footsteps echoed where no living soul trod, and whispers were carried through the air, their words unintelligible but laced with an otherworldly presence. The Elks Lodge, once a place of camaraderie, morphed into a realm where the living shared their space with restless spirits.

As the supernatural occurrences escalated, some members dared to investigate the haunted history of the Elks Lodge. Among them was Maggie, a fearless paranormal investigator who sought to unravel the mysteries that clung to the lodge like an unseen shroud. Armed with spectral detection equipment and a determination to uncover the truth, Maggie embarked on

The lodge. *Neal Parks Photography.*

a chilling journey through the dimly lit corridors and abandoned rooms. She encountered apparitions of forlorn souls and heard disembodied voices recounting tales of unfinished business.

However, the darker entities, drawn by the chaos unleashed by the mediums of the past, stirred in the hidden corners of the Elks Lodge. Unseen eyes glared from the shadows, and malevolent whispers taunted Maggie as she ventured deeper into the haunted recesses. In a climactic confrontation, Maggie faced the full force of the supernatural entities that had been awakened. The spirits, trapped in a vortex of unresolved energy, yearned for release, while the demons resisted, feeding off the fear that permeated the lodge.

With unyielding courage, Maggie employed a prayer to restore balance. The Elks Lodge, a battleground between the living and the dead, resonated with the echoes of a spiritual struggle. As the rituals took effect, the malevolent entities were banished, leaving the benevolent spirits to find peace. The Elks Lodge, forever marked by its haunted history, underwent a transformation. Maggie's efforts brought closure to the tormented souls, and the shadows that once clung to the property dissipated. The members of the lodge, now aware of the delicate balance between realms, carried the legacy of a chilling chapter in Chillicothe's supernatural history.

THE DEAD WON'T LET GO

In the heart of historical Frankfort, Ohio, a cluster of apartments stood sentinel, shadows lingering where once tombstones marked the resting places of the departed. Unbeknownst to many, these apartments were constructed on the hallowed ground of a family cemetery, and the spirits that slept beneath the earth were far from at peace. Tom, unaware of the cemetery's history, moved into the apartments by the school with the optimism of a new resident. The initial excitement waned as peculiar occurrences began to unfold. Strange whispers echoed through the halls, and the air seemed to carry the weight of unseen eyes.

As Tom settled into his routine, he became increasingly aware of the spectral inhabitants that coexisted with the living. Shadows flickered in the periphery of his vision, and the temperature dropped inexplicably when he walked past certain corners. Unease settled in his gut, and restless nights became the norm. Late one evening, Tom, drawn by an otherworldly pull, ventured into the building's basement. To his horror, he discovered remnants of the old cemetery, forgotten beneath the concrete foundation. The gravestones, once standing tall, now lay toppled and shattered, an eerie testament to the disrupted peace of the departed.

From that moment on, the ghosts manifested with an unsettling intensity. Tom would catch glimpses of spectral figures lingering by his window at night, their ethereal forms casting a haunting glow. Whispers escalated into mournful wails that echoed through the apartment complex, carrying tales of lives cut short and a final resting place desecrated. The spirits seemed anchored to the apartments, their presence an unwavering force that refused to dissipate. Desperation clawed at Tom as he struggled to coexist with the restless souls that wandered the halls. Attempts to communicate with the apparitions were met with fleeting glimpses and ominous silhouettes.

As time passed, the spectral activity reached a crescendo. Tom, worn down by the relentless haunting, sought the help of local paranormal investigators. Together, they conducted séances and rituals, attempting to offer solace to the aggrieved spirits. Yet the ghosts, bound by a sorrowful history, resisted the call to move on. The apartments by the school became a realm where the living and the dead converged, a haunting testament to the consequences of disturbing sacred ground. Tom, forever changed by his four years in the spectral presence, left with an awareness that the departed had woven their ethereal threads into the very fabric of the apartments, leaving an indelible mark on the haunted grounds of Frankfort.

ABOUT THE AUTHOR

Neal Parks is the author of seven books, including *Haunted Holidays, Haunted Chillicothe* and *Paranormal Chronicles*. He's also written and narrated an audiobook titled *Neal Parks Presents Terrifying Tales to Tell Your Friends*. He's coauthored two more books, including *Blood Alley Stories*, and is an illustrator of children's books. He lives in Chillicothe with his amazing family and four adorable dogs. If you'd like to learn more about Neal Parks, check out the following links:

https://nealparks.univer.se
https://www.amazon.com/stores/Neal-Parks/author
https://www.lulu.com/spotlight/nealparks
https://nealparks.bandcamp.com/album/neal-parks-presents-truly-
    terrifying-tales

Neal is also available for contact through Facebook, YouTube, Instagram, TikTok and LinkedIn. You are more than welcome to email him (thenealparks@gmail.com).

FREE eBOOK OFFER

Scan the QR code below, enter your e-mail address and get our original Haunted America compilation eBook delivered straight to your inbox for free.

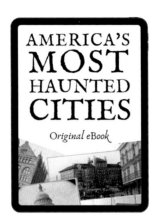

ABOUT THE BOOK

Every city, town, parish, community and school has their own paranormal history. Whether they are spirits caught in the Bardo, ancestors checking on their descendants, restless souls sending a message or simply spectral troublemakers, ghosts have been part of the human tradition from the beginning of time.

In this book, we feature a collection of stories from five of America's most haunted cities: Baltimore, Chicago, Galveston, New Orleans and Washington, D.C.

SCAN TO GET
AMERICA'S MOST HAUNTED CITIES

Having trouble scanning? Go to:
biz.arcadiapublishing.com/americas-most-haunted-cities